STUDY GUIDE

INDIANA CHRISTIAN UNIVERSITY

THE ACTS
OF THE APOSTLES

by
DR. LESTER SUMRALL

Sumrall Publishing
P. O. Box 12
South Bend, IN 46624

PLEASE NOTE:

This study guide is designed to be a companion to the audio/video teaching tape, *The Acts of the Apostles*, by Dr. Lester Sumrall.

It is a college workbook with space allowed for your personal notes.

All scriptures, unless otherwise indicated, are taken from the *King James Version of the Holy Bible*.

Scripture quotations marked AMP are taken from the *Amplified Bible*, Copyright 1965 by Zondervan Publishing House, Grand Rapids, MI.

Scripture quotations marked NKJV are taken from the *New King James Version of the Bible*, Copyright 1983 by Thomas Nelson Publishers, Nashville, TN.

Audio and videotapes are available from Sumrall Publishing.

Copyright © All Rights Reserved
Reprinted September, 2001

THE ACTS OF THE APOSTLES:
THE BIRTH OF THE CHRISTIAN CHURCH
ISBN 0-937580-92-9

Printed by Sumrall Publishing
P.O. Box 12
South Bend, Indiana 46624
www.sumrallpublishing.com

STUDY GUIDE

INDIANA CHRISTIAN UNIVERSITY

THE ACTS OF THE APOSTLES

TABLE OF CONTENTS

STUDY GUIDE

INDIANA CHRISTIAN UNIVERSITY

THE ACTS OF THE APOSTLES

Lesson 1

FACTS OF ACTS

INTRODUCTION:

The Acts of the Apostles contains the blueprint of the spiritual structure of the Church until Christ returns. The functioning of the gifts of the Spirit is the directing force of this great story. We could call this "The Acts of the Church."

READING:

Acts 1:1-2, *The former treatise have I made, O Theophilus, of all that Jesus began both to do and teach,*
v. 2, *Until the day in which he was taken up, after that he through the Holy Ghost had given commandments unto the apostles whom he had chosen:*

1. FACTS ABOUT THE BOOK

    A.   The author of The Acts of the Apostles is Luke, the beloved physician, who traveled with Paul.

    B.   Acts is the fifth book of the New Testament.

    C.   It is the 44th book of the Bible.

    D.   Although there are 38 chapters of Acts, the book has no written conclusion.

    E.   The book of Acts has 1,007 verses in the King James Version.

    F.   Acts has 24,250 words in the King James Version.

    G.   The book of Acts asks 75 questions.

    H.   Acts fulfills 21 Old Testament prophesies.

    I.   It describes 50 different operations of the gifts of the Holy Spirit.

2. TIME PERIOD

    A. It is remarkable that the book of Acts covers a period of approximately 32 years. (Dr. C.I. Scofield)

    B. The lifespan of The Acts of the Apostles is almost equal to the lifespan of Jesus Christ on Planet Earth.

        1) The lifespan of Christ brought salvation to the human race.

        2) The first Church generation turned the world upside down.

        Acts 17:6, And when they found them not, they drew Jason and certain brethren unto the rulers of the city, crying, These that have turned the world upside down are come hither also.

3. THE DIVISION OF ACTS

    A. Peter's leadership

    The first eight chapters describe the Jews at Jerusalem, their headquarters.

    B. Paul's leadership

    The last 20 chapters outline the Gentile's ordination, and the spread of the Church from Jerusalem to Rome. The city of Antioch was a hub of activity. One third of the last chapters is related to the accusations against Paul, his arrest and imprisonment in Rome.

4. WAS THERE A PATTERN FOR SUCCESS IN THE ACTS OF THE APOSTLES FOR THE BODY OF CHRIST?

    A. The Word of God was the basis.

        1) Peter preached the Old Testament at Pentecost.

        2) Stephen preached from the Old Testament at his martyrdom.

        3) Paul always spoke from biblical authority.

    B. The name of Jesus was the authority of the Church. The Church used the name of Christ to cast out devils, raise the dead, and heal the sick.

C.   The in-filling of the Holy Spirit was the key.

From the moment the sound of a rushing mighty wind came from heaven and the fire of God began to burn upon the apostles, these two vehicles of wind and fire have represented the strength and power to destroy pagan rituals, demolish demon doctrines, and bring truth and eternal life to multitudes of people.

Acts 2:3-4, *And there appeared unto them cloven tongues like as of fire, and it sat upon each of them.*
v. 4, *And they were all filled with the Holy Ghost, and began to speak with other tongues, as the Spirit gave them utterance.*

5.   WORD OF WISDOM

    A.   A word of wisdom was spoken by Jesus. Because He knew the disciples needed the baptism of the Holy Spirit, Jesus warned the disciples not to leave Jerusalem until they had it.

Acts 1:4-5, *And, being assembled together with them, commanded them that they should not depart from Jerusalem, but wait for the promise of the Father, which, saith he, ye have heard of me.*
v. 5, *For John truly baptized with water; but ye shall be baptized with the Holy Ghost not many days hence.*

    B.   Christ gave another word of wisdom. This baptism would be an anointing of power to make the disciples bold witnesses of Jesus.

Acts 1:8, *But ye shall receive power, after that the Holy Ghost is come upon you: and ye shall be witnesses unto me both in Jerusalem, and in all Judæa, and in Samaria, and unto the uttermost part of the earth.*

    C.   Christ declared another word of wisdom. Jesus foretold that special manifestations would follow.

Mark 16:15-17, *And he said unto them, Go ye into all the world, and preach the gospel to every creature.*
v. 16, *He that believeth and is baptized shall be saved; but he that believeth not shall be damned.*
v. 17, *And these signs shall follow them that believe; In my name shall they cast out devils; they shall speak with new tongues.*

6.   THE PROPHETIC BIRTH

The prophet Isaiah predicted the birth of the Church:

A.   Isaiah 32:4, *The heart also of the rash shall understand knowledge, and the tongue of the stammerers shall be ready to speak plainly.*

This was some 700 years before fulfillment came.

B.   Isaiah 28:9-11, *Whom shall he teach knowledge? and whom shall he make to understand doctrine? them that are weaned from the milk, and drawn from the breasts.*
v. 10, *For precept must be upon precept, precept upon precept; line upon line, line upon line; here a little, and there a little:*
v. 11, *For with stammering lips and another tongue will he speak to this people.*

7.   APOSTLES AWAITED FULFILLMENT

The apostles and the rest of the 120 waiting in the Upper Room in Jerusalem knew these prophesies and eagerly awaited the divine fulfillment:

A.   The voice from heaven

B.   The rushing mighty wind

C.   The divine fire

This rested upon the heads of those who became the pillars and foundations of the glorious and conquering Church of the Lord Jesus Christ.

STUDY GUIDE

INDIANA CHRISTIAN UNIVERSITY

THE ACTS OF THE APOSTLES

Lesson 2

A NEW THING PREDICTED

INTRODUCTION:

The book of Acts is a *sequel* to the four gospels. It begins with 40 days of infallible proofs of Christ's resurrection.

READING:

Acts 1:3, *To whom also he shewed himself alive after his passion by many infallible proofs, being seen of them forty days, and speaking of the things pertaining to the kingdom of God.*

1. THE DIVINE SEQUEL

Acts 1:1-2, 4, *The former treatise have I made, O Theophilus, of all that Jesus began both to do and teach,*
v. 2, *Until the day in which he was taken up, after that he through the Holy Ghost had given commandments unto the apostles whom he had chosen:*

v. 4, *And, being assembled together with them, commanded them that they should not depart from Jerusalem, but wait for the promise of the Father, which, saith he, ye have heard of me.*

Theophilus, though an unknown believer to us, must have been a prominent man. The Acts of the Apostles was addressed to him, and Luke said that he was an excellent person. Luke wrote the most complete biography of Jesus of the four apostles.

2. COMMANDMENTS SENT TO THE CHOSEN

Although Jesus was now taken up to heaven, God could give directions to His disciples through the Holy Ghost. Acts 1:2, *. . .that he through the Holy Ghost had given commandments unto the apostles whom he had chosen.*

3. FORTY DAYS OF INFALLIBLE PROOFS

The New Testament records various appearances of the Lord to men and women, proving his resurrection. He ate and drank with them, and they touched His hands and feet and heard His voice.

Acts 1:3, *To whom also he shewed himself alive after his passion by many infallible proofs, being seen of them forty days, and speaking of the things pertaining to the kingdom of God.*

A. To Mary of Magdalene

Mark 16:9-11, *Now when Jesus was risen early the first day of the week, he appeared first to Mary Magdalene, out of whom he had cast seven devils.*
v. 10, *And she went and told them that had been with him, as they mourned and wept.*
v. 11, *And they, when they had heard that he was alive, and had been seen of her, believed not.*

B. To the other women

Matthew 28:1-10, *In the end of the sabboth, as it began to dawn toward the first day of the week, came Mary Magdalene and the other Mary to see the sepulchre.* Gabriel (?)
v. 2, *And, behold, there was a great earthquake: for the angel of the Lord descended from heaven, and came and rolled back the stone from the door and sat upon it.*
v. 3, *His countenance was like lightening, and his raiment white as snow:*
v. 4, *And for fear of him the keepers did shake, and became as dead men.*
v. 5, *And the angel answered and said unto the women, Fear not ye: for I know that ye seek Jesus, which was crucified.*
v. 6, *He is not here: for he is risen, as he said. Come, see the place where the Lord lay.*
v. 7, *And go quickly, and tell his disciples that he is risen, from the dead; and, behold, he goeth before you into Galilee; there shall you see him: lo, I have told you.*

v. 8, *And they departed quickly from the sepulchre with fear and great joy; and did run to bring his disciples word..*
v. 9, *And as they went to tell his disciples, behold, Jesus met them, saying, All hail. And they came and held him by the feet, and worshipped him.*
v. 10, *Then said Jesus unto them, Be not afraid: go tell my brethren that they go into Galilee, and there shall they see me.*

C. To Peter

Luke 24:34, *Saying, The Lord is risen indeed, and hath appeared to Simon.*

D. To the disciples on the road to Emmaus

Mark 16:12-13, *After that he appeared in another form unto two of them, as they walked, and went into the country.*
v. 13, *And they went and told it unto the residue: neither believed they them.*

Luke 24:13, *And, behold, two of them went that same day to a village called Emmaus, which was from Jerusalem about threescore furlongs.*

Luke 24:25-31, *Then he said unto them, O fools, and slow of heart to believe all that the prophets have spoken:*
v. 26, *Ought not Christ to have suffered these things, and to enter into his glory?*
v. 27, *And beginning at Moses and all the prophets, he expounded unto them in all the scriptures the things concerning himself.*
v. 28, *And they drew nigh unto the village, whither they went: and he made as though he would have gone further.*
v. 29, *But they constrained him, saying, Abide with us: for it is toward evening, and the day is far spent. And he went in to tarry with them.*
v. 30, *And it came to pass, as he sat at meat with them, he took bread, and blessed it, and brake, and gave to them.*
v. 31, *And their eyes were opened, and they knew him: and he vanished out of their sight.*

E. To all the disciples except Thomas

John 20:19-20, *Then the same day at evening, being the first day of the week, when the doors were shut where the disciples were assembled for fear of the Jews, came Jesus and stood in the midst, and saith unto them, Peace be unto you.*
v. 20, *And when he had so said, he shewed unto them his hands and his side. Then were the disciples glad, when they saw the Lord.*

F.   To all the disciples including Thomas

John 20:26-28, *And after eight days again his disciples were within, and Thomas with them: then came Jesus, the doors being shut, and stood in the midst, and said, Peace be into you.*
v. 27, *Then saith he to Thomas, Reach hither thy finger, and behold my hands; and reach hither thy hand, and thrust it into my side: and be not faithless, but believing.*
v. 28, *And Thomas answered and said unto him, My Lord and my God.*

John 20:30-31, *And many other signs truly did Jesus in the presence of his disciples, which are not written in this book:*
v. 31, *But these are written, that ye might believe that Jesus is the Christ, the Son of God; and that believing ye might have life through his name.*

G.   To the eleven disciples in Galilee

Matthew 28:16-17, *Then the eleven disciples went away into Galilee, into a mountain where Jesus had appointed them.*
v. 17, *And when they saw him, they worshipped him: but some doubted.*

H.   To all the disciples and others

Luke 24:36-40, *And as they thus spake, Jesus himself stood in the midst of them, and saith unto them, Peace be unto you.*
v. 37, *But they were terrified and affrighted, and supposed that they had seen a spirit.*
v. 38, *And he said unto them, Why are ye troubled? and why do thoughts arise in your hearts?*
v. 39, *Behold my hands and my feet, that it is I myself: handle me, and see; for a spirit hath not flesh and bones, as ye see me have.*
v. 40, *And when he had thus spoken, he shewed them his hands and feet.*

I.   To seven disciples at the Sea of Galilee

John 21:1-2, 12-13, *After these things Jesus shewed himself again to the disciples at the sea of Tiberias; and on this wise shewed himself.*
v. 2, *There were together Simon Peter, and Thomas called Didymus, and Nathanael of Cana in Galilee,a nd the sons of Zebedee, and two other of his disciples.*

v. 12, *Jesus saith unto them, Come and dine. And none of the disciples durst ask him, Who art thou? knowing that it was the Lord.*
v. 13, *Jesus then cometh, and taketh bread, and giveth them, and fish likewise.*

J.   To over 500 disciples on a mountain

I Corinthians 15:6, *After that, he was seen of above five hundred brethren at once; of whom the greater part remain unto this present, but some are fallen asleep.*

K.   To James

I Corinthians 15:7, *After that, he was seen of James; then of all the apostles.*

L.   To all the disciples at His ascension

Mark 16:14-20, *Afterward he appeared unto the eleven as they sat at meat, and upbraided them with their unbelief and hardness of heart, because they believed not them which had seen him after he was risen.*
v. 15, *And he said unto them, Go ye into all the world, and preach the gospel to every creature.*
v. 16, *He that believeth and is baptized shall be saved; but he that believeth not shall be damned.*
v. 17, *And these signs shall follow them that believe: In my name shall they cast out devils; they shall speak with new tongues;*
v. 18, *They shall take up serpents; and if they drink any deadly thing, it shall not hurt them; they shall lay hands on the sick, and they shall recover.*
v. 19, *So then after the Lord had spoken unto them, he was received up into heaven, and sat on the right hand of God.*
v. 20, *And they went forth, and preached everywhere, the Lord working with them, and confirming the word with signs following: Amen.*

Luke 24:51, *And it came to pass, while he blessed them, he was parted from them, and carried up into heaven.*

4.   JESUS COMMANDS THE CHURCH TO BE BORN IN JERUSALEM

Before He departed from the disciples, Jesus specifically ordered them to remain in Jerusalem until they received the Father's promise of power.

Acts 1:4, *And, being assembled together with them, commanded them that they should not depart from Jerusalem, but wait for the promise of the Father, which, saith he, ye have heard of me.*

13

5.   PROPHECY OF THE COMING OF HOLY GHOST BAPTISM

Acts 1:5, *For John truly baptized with water; but ye shall be baptized with the Holy Ghost not many days hence.*

The change or transition from the personal leadership of Christ in the four gospels to the leadership of the Person of the Holy Ghost, known as the Third Person of the Trinity, occurs in the book of the Acts of the Apostles.

STUDY GUIDE

INDIANA CHRISTIAN UNIVERSITY

THE ACTS OF THE APOSTLES

Lesson 3

THE FIRST DAY OF THE CHURCH

INTRODUCTION:

The first happenings in the apostolic Church are the heart of the Christian message. These events materialized in the first part of the book of Acts.

Acts show God's concern over His newly established church. These initial activities set a pattern for the entire church age or dispensation. Also, they reveal the secret of grace.

READING:

Acts 2:14, *But Peter, standing up with the eleven, lifted up his voice, and said unto them, Ye men of Judæa, and all ye that dwell at Jerusalem, be this known unto you, and hearken to my words.*

1. PENTECOST WAS A TRADITIONAL FESTIVAL

    A. It began with Moses and was part of the Law.

    B. It brought multitudes to Jerusalem each year.

        Acts 2:5, *And there were dwelling at Jerusalem Jews, devout men, out of every nation under heaven.*

    C. It marked the completion of the wheat harvest, and was the 50th day after the Festival of Passover.

    D. The Feast of Pentecost had become associated with rituals promoted by the scribes and Pharisees.

    E. It was to be a time of national rejoicing.

2.   AWAITING THE HOLY SPIRIT

A.   The disciples tarried in the Upper Room in obedience to Christ's command.

Luke 24:49, *And, behold, I send the promise of my Father upon you: but tarry ye in the city of Jerusalem, until ye be endued with the power from on high.*

Acts 2:1, *And when the day of Pentecost was fully come, they were all with one accord in one place.*

B.   The 120 remained faithful while waiting for the fulfillment of divine promises.

C.   They filled approximately ten days with praise, prayer and supplication.

3.   HIS COMING FULFILLED

A.   A manifestation of the divine presence settled on the disciples.

Acts 2:3, *And there appeared unto them cloven tongues like as of fire, and it sat upon each of them.*

B.   The Spirit personally took control of their bodies.

Acts 2:4, *And they were all filled with the Holy Ghost, and began to speak with other tongues, as the Spirit gave them utterance.*

4.   THE CROWD WAS ATTRACTED AND AMAZED

A.   The sound of wind may have stirred some attention.

Acts 2:2, *And suddenly there came a sound from heaven as of a rushing mighty wind, and it filled all the house where they were sitting.*

B.   Speaking in tongues really drew them.

Acts 2:6, *Now when this was noised abroad, the multitude came together, and were confounded, because that every man heard them speak in his own language.*

C.   The crowd saw that something supernatural was present.

Acts 2:7, *And they were all amazed and marvelled, saying one to another, Behold, are not these which speak Galilæans?*

D.   Many from different parts of the world understood the languages. No interpretation was needed.

Acts 2:8, *And how hear we every man in our own tongue, wherein we were born?*

E.   The disciples spoke like natives without a Galilean accent.

Acts 2:9-12, *Parthians, and Medes, and Elamites, and the dwellers in Mesopotamia, and in Judæa, and Cappadocia, in Pontus, and Asia,*
v. 10, *Phrygia, and Pamphylia, in Egypt, and in the parts of Libya about Cyrene, and strangers of Rome, Jews and proselytes,*
v. 11, *Cretes and Arabians, we do hear them speak in our tongues the wonderful works of God.*
v. 12, *And they were all amazed, and were in doubt, saying one to another, What meaneth this?*

F.   The crowd accused them of drunkenness.

Acts 2:13, *Others mocking said, These men are full of new wine.*

5.   PETER ANSWERS

A.   He first dealt with the mockers.

Acts 2:15, *For these are not drunken, as ye suppose, seeing it is but the third hour of the day.*

B.   Then he gave a quotation from Joel's prophecy.

Acts 2:16-21, *But this is that which was spoken by the prophet Joel;*
v. 17, *And it shall come to pass in the last days, saith God, I will pour out of my Spirit upon all flesh: and your sons and your daughters shall prophesy, and your young men shall see visions, and your old men shall dream dreams:*
v. 18, *And on my servants and on my handmaidens I will pour out in those days of my Spirit; and they shall prophesy:*

17

> v. 19, *And I will show wonders in heaven above, and signs in the earth beneath; blood, and fire, and vapour of smoke:*
> v. 20, *The sun shall be turned into darkness, and the moon into blood, before that great and notable day of the Lord come:*
> v. 21, *And it shall come to pass, that whosoever shall call upon the name of the Lord shall be saved.*

C. Next he uttered a message understandable to the crowd.

> Acts 2:22-23, *Ye men of Israel, hear these words; Jesus of Nazareth, a man approved of God among you by miracles and wonders and signs, which God did by him in the midst of you, as ye yourselves also know:*
> v. 23, *Him, being delivered by the determinate counsel and foreknowledge of God, ye have taken, and by wicked hands have crucified and slain.*

6. UNIVERSAL INVITATION

A. It is for all flesh; there are no limitations.

> Acts 2:37-38, *Now when they heard this, they were pricked in their heart, and said unto Peter and to the rest of the apostles, Men and brethren, what shall we do?*
> v. 38, *Then Peter said unto them, Repent, and be baptized every one of you in the name of Jesus Christ for the remission of sins, and ye shall receive the gift of the Holy Ghost.*

B. God calls whosoever will listen. All humanity is included in God's call.

> Acts 2:39, *For the promise is unto you, and to your children, and to all that are afar off, even as many as the Lord shall call.*

INDIANA CHRISTIAN UNIVERSITY

THE ACTS OF THE APOSTLES

Lesson 4

NEW TONGUES FOR NEW PEOPLE

INTRODUCTION:

God has given a beautiful gift from the Holy Spirit, but it has become one of the most controversial topics in the Church today.

READING:

Acts 2:4, *And they were all filled with the Holy Ghost, and began to speak with other tongues, as the Spirit gave them utterance.*

1. RECEIVING THE HOLY SPIRIT BAPTISM IS DIFFERENT FROM RECEIVING THE SPIRIT AT SALVATION.

    A. The disciples at Pentecost already were intimate with Christ and His Spirit.

    B. They received a separate experience in the Upper Room on that first Pentecost.

2. THIS EXPERIENCE IS NOT JUST AN ISOLATED EVENT FOR THE DAY OF PENTECOST.

    A. Some did receive this on the Day of Pentecost.

    Acts 2:38, *Then Peter said unto them, Repent, and be baptized every one of you in the name of Jesus Christ for the remission of sins, and ye shall receive the gift of the Holy Ghost.*
    v. 41, *Then they that gladly received his word were baptized: and the same day there were added unto them about three thousand souls.*

    B.   However, the believers at Cornelius' house received this experience some 10 years later.

          Acts 10:46, *For they heard them speak with tongues, and magnify God . .*

    C.   The disciples at Ephesus received it some 20 years later.

          Acts 19:6, *And when Paul had laid his hands upon them, the Holy Ghost came on them; and they spake with tongues, and prophesied.*

    D.   This experience is widespread even today.

2. THE EXPERIENCE OF SPEAKING IN TONGUES IS TO BE HONORED AND COVETED.

    A.   I Corinthians 14:18, *I thank my God that I speak in tongues more than ye all.*

    B.   I Corinthians 14:39, *Wherefore, brethren, covet to prophesy, and forbid not to speak with tongues.*

3. THE EXPERIENCE OF SPEAKING IN TONGUES WAS WIDESPREAD IN THE EARLY CHURCH.

    A.   Acts 2:4, *And they were filled with the Holy Ghost, and began to speak with other tongues, as the Spirit gave them utterance.*

    B.   I Corinthians 12:10, *To another the working of miracles; to another prophesy, to another discerning of spirits; to another divers kinds of tongues; to another the interpretation of tongues.*

    C.   I Corinthians 12:28, *And God hath set some in the church, first apostles, secondarily prophets, thirdly teachers, after that miracles, then gifts of healings, helps, governments, diversities of tongues.*

    D.   In the early Church speaking in tongues publicly was such a common occurrence that Paul needed to establish guidelines for its use.

          I Corinthians 14:26-28, *How is it then, brethren? when ye come together, every one of you hath a psalm, hath a doctrine, hath a tongue, hath a revelation, hath an interpretation. Let all things be done unto edifying.*
v. 27, If any man speak in an unknown tongue, let it be by two, or at the most by three, and that by course; and let one interpret.
v. 28, But if there be no interpreter, let him keep silence in the church; and let him speak to himself, and to God.

5. SPEAKING IN TONGUES IS NOT "GIBBERRISH," BUT PRAISE TO GOD.

    Acts 2:11, *Cretes and Arabians, we do hear them speak in our tongues the wonderful works of God.*

6. TONGUES ARE A SOURCE OF POWER.

    A. It builds up the individual believer.

        I Corinthians 14:4, *He that speaketh in an unknown tongue edifieth himself; but he that prophesieth edifieth the church.*

    B. It builds up the Church.

        I Corinthians 14:5, *I would that ye all spake with tongues, but rather that ye prophesied: for greater is he that prophesieth than he that speaketh with tongues, except he interpret, that the church may receive edifying.*

7. TONGUES ARE DIRECTED TO GOD

    I Corinthians 14:2, *For he that speaketh in an unknown tongue speaketh not unto men, but unto God: for no man understandeth him; howbeit in the spirit he speaketh mysteries.*

8. TONGUES ARE OF THE SPIRIT, NOT OF THE SOUL OF MAN.

    I Corinthians 14:14, *For if I pray in an unknown tongue, my spirit prayeth, but my understanding is unfruitful.*

9. TONGUES ARE FOR A SIGN TO UNBELIEVERS

    I Corinthians 14:22, *Wherefore tongues are for a sign, not to them that believe, but to them that believeth not: but prophesying serveth not for them that believe not, but for them which believe.*

NOTES

_____

_____

_____

_____

_____

_____

_____

_____

_____

_____

_____

_____

_____

_____

_____

_____

_____

_____

_____

_____

_____

_____

_____

_____

_____

_____

_____

_____

STUDY GUIDE

INDIANA CHRISTIAN UNIVERSITY

THE ACTS OF THE APOSTLES

Lesson 5

SPIRITUAL GIFTS MANIFESTED AT THE BIRTH OF THE CHURCH

INTRODUCTION:

On the day the Church was born, three gifts (one from each category for the gifts) were demonstrated through the Church.

READING:

Acts 2:16, *But this is that which was spoken of by the prophet Joel.*

1. GIFTS OF THE SPIRIT WERE IN OPERATION IN THIS SECOND CHAPTER OF ACTS.

    A. The gift of speaking in various kinds of tongues

        1) This beginning of gifts is significant.

        2) Acts 2:1, *And when the day of Pentecost was fully come, they were all with one accord in one place.*

            a) God is always on schedule. He is never late.
            b) "They" indicates the right people: the ready ones were there.
            c) "All" is indicative of the sovereignty of God.
            d) "One place" denotes unity and strength.

        3) Acts 2:2, *And suddenly there came a sound from heaven as of a rushing mighty wind, and it filled all the house where they were sitting.*

- a) "Suddenly" reminds us that great events are often unannounced. History is often abrupt.
- b) "Sound"--This was a sound from God, not from any man.
- c) The sound came "from heaven," not from earth.
- d) "Filled" describes the entire place from back to front.
- e) "All the house" is notable because the Church begins in the home.
- f) "Sitting"--There are no holy postures. It is not the position of the body, but the condition of the spirit that counts.

4) Acts 2:3, *And there appeared unto them cloven tongues like as of fire, and it sat upon each of them.*

   "Tongues of fire" denotes cleansing or devouring.

5) Acts 2:4, *And they were all filled with the Holy Ghost, and began to speak with other tongues, as the Spirit gave them utterance.*

   - a) "All filled" states that not one person was left out.
   - b) The Holy Ghost or Spirit was given to everyone--not just the apostles.
   - c) They spoke in other languages. It was a supernatural utterance with the natural tongue, lips, and throat.
   - d) Tongues is an utterance of the spirit, not of the mind or soul.

      I Corinthians 14:14, *For if I pray in an unknown tongue, my spirit prayeth, but my understanding is unfruitful.*

      John 7:38, *He that believeth on me, as the scripture hath said, out of his belly shall flow rivers of living water.*

B. The gift of the word of wisdom operated through Peter.

   Acts 2:38-39, *Then Peter said unto them, Repent, and be baptized every one of you in the name of Jesus Christ for the remission of sins, and ye shall receive the gift of the Holy Ghost.*
   v. 39, *For the promise is unto you, and to your children, and to all that are afar off, even as many as the Lord our God shall call.*

   1) It is for those present.
   2) It is for the following generation, even for your children.
   3) It is for those far off, with no limit in time.
   4) As many as are called to salvation can receive the in-filling of the Holy Spirit.

C. The gifts of healing

Acts 2:43, *And fear came upon every soul: and many wonders and signs were done by the apostles.*

2. THE FRUIT OF THE SPIRIT WAS MANIFESTED IN THIS SAME CHAPTER.

A. Unselfishness

Although these believers were later dispersed throughout the world by Roman decree, they lost nothing.

Acts 2:44-45, *And all that believed were together, and had all things common. v. 45, And sold their possessions and goods, and parted them to all men, as every man had need.*

B. Gladness of heart

Acts 2:46-47, *And they, continuing daily with one accord in the temple, and breaking bread from house to house, did eat their meat with gladness and singleness of heart,*
v. 47, Praising God, and having favour with all the people. And the Lord added to the church daily such as should be saved.

NOTES

_____

_____

_____

_____

_____

_____

_____

_____

_____

_____

_____

_____

_____

_____

_____

_____

_____

_____

_____

_____

_____

_____

_____

STUDY GUIDE

INDIANA CHRISTIAN UNIVERSITY

THE ACTS OF THE APOSTLES

Lesson 6

THE PROMISE IS UNTO YOU

INTRODUCTION:

The Holy Spirit has been active throughout human history. The Old Testament and the New Testament testify to His continual operations.

READING:

Acts 2:38-39, *Then Peter said unto them, Repent, and be baptized every one of you in the name of Jesus Christ for the remission of sins, and ye shall receive the gift of the Holy Ghost.*
v. 39, *For the promise is unto you, and to your children, and to all that are afar off, even as many as the Lord shall call.*

1.   HE CAN QUICKEN, OR MAKE ALIVE

    A.   The words of God bring life.

        John 6:63, *It is the spirit that quickeneth; the flesh profiteth nothing: the words that I speak unto you, they are spirit, and they are life.*

    B.   He can renew those who are bound by sins.

        Ephesians 2:1, *And you hath he quickened, who were dead in trespasses and sins.*

    C.   The Holy Spirit not only reveals the meaning of God's words, He also makes them come alive in your spirit.

        II Corinthians 3:6, *Who also hath made us able ministers of the new testament; not of the letter, but of the spirit: for the letter killeth, but the spirit giveth life.*

2.   HE CAN RENEW YOU

A.   The Holy Spirit restores us because God is merciful.

Titus 3:5, *Not by works of righteousness which we have done, but according to his mercy he saved us, by the washing of regeneration, and renewing of the Holy Ghost.*

B.   He can rejuvenate our minds.

Ephesians 4:23, *And be renewed in the spirit of your mind.*

3.   HE CAN STRENGTHEN YOU

A.   His power fortifies your spirit man.

Ephesians 3:16, *That he would grant you, according to the riches of his glory, to be strengthened with might by his Spirit in the inner man.*

4.   HE SANCTIFIES YOU

The Holy Spirit sets you apart for a sacred purpose. He purifies you, freeing you from sin, efficiently making you a means of holiness.

A.   II Thessalonians 2:13, *But we are bound to give thanks alway to God for you, brethren beloved of the Lord, because God hath from the beginning chosen you to salvation through sanctification of the Spirit and belief of the truth.*

B.   Romans 15:16, *That I should be the minister of Jesus Christ to the Gentiles, ministering the gospel of God, that the offering up of the Gentiles might be acceptable, being sanctified by the Holy Ghost.*

C.   I Peter 1:2, *Elect according to the foreknowledge of God the Father, through sanctification of the Spirit, unto obedience and sprinkling of the blood of Jesus Christ: Grace unto you, and peace, be multiplied.*

D.   I Corinthians 6:11, *And such were some of you: but ye are washed, but ye are sanctified, but ye are justified in the name of the Lord Jesus, and by the Spirit of our God.*

E.   Galatians 5:16, *This I say then, Walk in the Spirit, and ye shall not fulfill the lust of the flesh.*

5. HE MAKES US INTO THE IMAGE OF JESUS CHRIST

II Corinthians 3:18, *But we all, with open face beholding as in a glass the glory of the Lord, are changed into the same image from glory to glory, even as by the Spirit of the Lord.*

6. HE CAN COMFORT AND GUIDE YOU

Strengthening you with knowledge and wisdom as you need it, the Holy Spirit will reliably direct your life.

A. John 16:13, *Howbeit when he, the Spirit of truth, is come, he will guide you into all truth: for he shall not speak of himself; but whatsoever he shall hear, that shall he speak: and he will shew you things to come.*

B. John 14:16-17, 26, *And I will pray the Father, and he shall give you another Comforter, that he may abide with you for ever;*
v. 17, Even the Spirit of truth; whom the world cannot receive, because it seeth him not, neither knoweth him: but ye know him; for he dwelleth with you, and shall be in you.
v. 26, But the Comforter, which is the Holy Ghost, whom the Father will send in my name, he shall teach you all things, and bring all things to your remembrance, whatsoever I have said unto you.

7. HE CAN GIVE YOU POWER

A. Authority is one form of power.

B. Energy is another form of power.

C. The Holy Spirit gives both authority and energy.

D. Acts 1:8, *But ye shall receive power, after that the Holy Ghost is come upon you: and ye shall be witnesses into me both is Jerusalem, and in all Judæa, and in Samaria, and unto the uttermost part of the earth.*

CONCLUSION:

We were born again by the Spirit.

We live by the Spirit.

We will be raptured by the Spirit.

NOTES

_____

_____

_____

_____

_____

_____

_____

_____

_____

_____

_____

_____

_____

_____

_____

_____

_____

_____

_____

_____

_____

_____

_____

_____

_____

STUDY GUIDE

INDIANA CHRISTIAN UNIVERSITY

THE ACTS OF THE APOSTLES

Lesson 7

THE FIRST APOSTOLIC MIRACLE

INTRODUCTION:

Pentecost brought with it the fulfillment of Jesus' words, which promised power to witness and to do greater works. On the days following, many wonders and signs were done by the apostles.

READING:

Acts 3:11-13, 16, *And as the lame man which was healed held Peter and John, all the people ran together unto them in the porch that is called Solomon's, greatly wondering.*
v. 12, *And when Peter saw it, he answered unto the people, Ye men of Israel, why marvel ye at this? or why look ye so earnestly on us, as though by our own power or holiness we had made this man to walk?*
v. 13, *The God of Abraham, and of Isaac, and of Jacob, the God of our fathers, hath glorified his Son Jesus. . .*
v. 16, *And his name through faith In his name hath made this man strong, whom ye see and know: yea, the faith which is by him hath given him this perfect soundness in the presence of you all.*

1.   A NEEDY LIFE

The disciples recognized a man in need.

Acts 3:1-2, *Now Peter and John went up together into the temple at the hour of prayer, being the ninth hour.*
v. 2, *And a certain man lame from his mother's womb was carried, whom they laid daily at the gate of the temple which is called Beautiful, to ask for alms of them that entered into the temple.*

The First Apostolic Miracle
Lesson 7

- A. Peter and John went to the temple at the hour of prayer.

- B. They encountered a cripple begging for charity.

- C. The disabled man was a challenge to the apostles.

- D. Pentecost was as real on the Temple steps as is was in the Upper Room.

2. THE NEED EXPRESSED

The helpless invalid asked for money for his existence.

Acts 3:3, *Who seeing Peter and John about to go into the temple asked an alms.*

- A. Instead of turning away, the disciples gave full attention to the man's request.

- B. Resigned to his condition, the beggar believed normal life was impossible for him.

- C. The apostles saw a need far deeper than the superficial gift of money could supply.

3. THE COMMAND OF FAITH

- A. Exercising his authority, Peter commanded the beggar's attention.

   Acts 3:4, *And Peter, fastening his eyes upon him with John, said, Look on us.*

- B. This request revealed wisdom, not pride.

- C. This beggar's expectant response opened the door.

   Acts 3:5, *And he gave heed unto them, expecting to receive something of them.*

4. THE MIRACLE OF HEALING

Acts 3:6-7, *Then Peter said, Silver and gold have I none; but such as I have give I thee: In the name of Jesus Christ of Nazareth rise up and walk.*
v. 7, And he took him by the right hand, and lifted him up: and immediately his feet and ankle bones received strength.

- A. Having given the command to walk, Peter raised the lame man up.

- B. Shriveled muscles and twisted bones became firm, strong and normal.

5. A COMPLETE HEALING

Because he believed he would receive something, the man was made whole and began to rejoice.

Acts 3:8, *And he leaping up stood, and walked, and entered with them into the temple, walking, and leaping, and praising God.*

A. Physical healing came by an act of faith.

B. Spiritual healing brought joy and strength.

6. AN ASTONISHING HEALING

The unexpected sight of the poor man upright on his feet caused astonishment and bewilderment in the people.

Acts 3:9-10, *And all the people saw him walking and praising God.*
v. 10, *And they knew that is was he which sat for alms at the Beautiful gate of the temple: and they were filled with wonder and amazement at that which had happened unto him.*

A. Loud shouts of "Hallelujah!" attracted a crowd who ran to catch a glimpse.

B. The beggar was readily recognized by those who often came to pray.

C. Rejoicing in his new-found love, the formerly lame man grasped Peter.

D. The apostles preached Christ to the astonished onlookers and exhorted them to repent.

NOTES

_____
_____
_____
_____
_____
_____
_____
_____
_____
_____
_____
_____
_____
_____
_____
_____
_____
_____
_____
_____
_____
_____
_____
_____
_____
_____

STUDY GUIDE

INDIANA CHRISTIAN UNIVERSITY

THE ACTS OF THE APOSTLES

Lesson 8

THE FIRST PERSECUTION

INTRODUCTION:

The healing of the lame beggar in chapter three of Acts gives us the background and occasion for the first persecution of the Church. The priests and Sadducees, attracted by the commotion, gathered around the fringes of the crowd and heard Peter charging the Jews with the rejection and murder of Jesus and proclaiming His resurrection. The apostles and probably the lame man were arrested.

READING:

Acts 4:2, *Being grieved that they taught the people, and preached through Jesus the resurrection from the dead.*

1. THE RESULTS OF THE HEALING

    A. The religious authorities demonstrated anger against the apostles and the man who was healed.

        Acts 4:1, *And as they spake unto the people, the priests, and the captain of the temple, and the Sadducees, came upon them.*

    B. Peter and John were arrested and were put in jail until the next day since it was already late.

        Acts 4:3, *And they laid hands on them, and put them in hold unto the next day: for it was now eventide.*

    C. Faith came to sinners that day, and many who heard the message believed.

        Acts 4:4, *Howbeit many of them which heard the word believed; and the number of the men was about five thousand.*

    D. If the men who were saved numbered 5,000, their wives and children might bring the number to a minimum of 20,000 converts.

2. THE WISDOM AND POWER OF GOD

A. This miracle and gift could have operated through Jesus when he had visited the Temple during His lifetime. However, there would have been no great ingathering of souls, for He did these things daily.

B. God's timing for miracles is overwhelming in significance.

3. A DISDAINFUL QUESTION

The Sanhedrin met to question the apostles.

Acts 4:7-12, *And when they had set them in the midst, they asked, By what power, or by what name, have ye done this?*
v. 8, *Then Peter, filled with the Holy Ghost, said unto them, Ye rulers of the people, and elders of Israel,*
v. 9, *If we this day be examined of the good deed done to the impotent man, by what means he is made whole,*
v, 10, *Be it known unto you all, and to all the people of Israel, that by the name of Jesus Christ of Nazareth, whom ye crucified, whom God raised from the dead, even by him doth this man stand here before you whole.*
v. 11, *This is the stone which was set at nought of you builders, which is become the head of the corner.*
v. 12, *Neither is there salvation in any other: for there is none other name under heaven given among men, whereby we must be saved.*

A. With a proud status of superiority, the Jews asked, "By what power. . . or name have you done this?"

B. The apostles were treated with contempt while under arrest.

C. Their crime was causing a disturbance in the Temple.

4. A FEARLESS TESTIMONY

The Pharisees professed to be builders for God, yet the disciples claimed these leaders had misjudged and rejected the head stone of the corner.

Psalm 118:22, *The stone which the builders refused is become the head stone of the corner.*

Matthew 21:42, *Jesus saith unto them, Did ye never read in the scriptures, The stone which the builders rejected, the same is become the head of the corner: this is the Lord's doing, and it is marvellous in our eyes?*

A.   Under direct inspiration of the Spirit, the apostles gave no defense, argument or apology.

B.   They declare that the name that healed the cripple was that of Jesus whom the Jews crucified.

C.   The power was the same that God used to raise Christ from the dead.

5.   UNPLEASANT MEMORIES

A.   Peter's boldness, clarity, and directness shocked them.

B.   The unschooled fishermen were recognized as Jesus' disciples both in learning and in spirit.

Acts 4:13, *Now when they saw the boldness of Peter and John, and perceived that they were unlearned and ignorant men, they marveled; and they took knowledge of them, that they had been with Jesus.*

6.   INDISPUTABLE EVIDENCE

A.   The healed man was standing straight and strong.

B.   The rulers, elders and scribes wanted to deny the miracle and stop the spreading of the gospel.

C.   However, the healing was immediate, complete and astonishing. It could not be refuted.

7.   THE APOSTLES HAD DEFIANT COURAGE

A.   Although the council threatened punishment for the disciples if they used the name of Jesus again, Peter and John refused to be intimidated.

Acts 4:18-21, *And they called them, and commanded them not to speak at all nor teach in the name of Jesus.*
v. 19, *But Peter and John answered and said unto them, Whether it be right in the sight of God to hearken unto you more than unto God, judge ye.*
v. 20, *For we cannot but speak the things which we have seen and heard.*
v. 21, *So when they had further threatened them, they let them go, finding nothing how they might punish them, because of the people: for all men glorified God for that which was done.*

        1)   Threats of the Sanhedrin failed to frighten them.

        2)   They had a defiant boldness, holding the warnings of the Jewish council in contempt.

B.   Immediately the disciples met with friends and took the matter before the Lord, asking for even more boldness to proclaim the Word of God.

Acts 4:29-31, *And now, Lord, behold their threatenings: and grant unto thy servants, that with all boldness they may speak thy word,*
v, 30, *By stretching forth thine hand to heal; and that signs and wonders may be done by the name of thy holy child Jesus.*
v. 31, *And when they had prayed, the place was shaken where they were assembled together; and they were all filled with the Holy Ghost, and they spake the word of God with boldness.*

God gave them a Spirit-filled liberty.

8.   FAITH AND MIRACLES WERE GIVEN TO THE APOSTLES

A.   The gift of faith is when God supernaturally does something for you.

B.   The working of miracles is when God supernaturally does something through you.

9.   RESULTS OF THE GIFTS OF POWER

A.   When the Church finished praying the place where they were meeting was shaken, and they were all filled with boldness (Acts 4:31).

B.   They continued with one mind and heart to live for Christ.

Acts 4:32, *And the multitude of them that believed were of one heart and of one soul: neither said any of them that aught of the things which he possessed was his own; but they had all things common.*

C.   With authority and eloquence the apostles gave witness of the resurrection.

Acts 4:33, *And with great power gave the apostles witness of the resurrection of the Lord Jesus: and great grace was upon them all.*

STUDY GUIDE

INDIANA CHRISTIAN UNIVERSITY

THE ACTS OF THE APOSTLES

Lesson 9

THE FIRST PUNISHED SIN

INTRODUCTION:

In our last lesson we studied how the Church was attacked by outside persecution. In this lesson we will deal with an attack from the inside. Nothing hinders the Gospel more than the determined sins of Christians. Let us be aware of Satan's attacks.

READING:

Acts 5:9-11, *Then Peter said unto her, How is it that ye have agreed together to tempt the Spirit of the Lord? behold, the feet of them which have buried thy husband are at the door, and shall carry thee out.*
v. 10, *Then fell she down straightway at his feet, and yielded up the ghost: and the young men came in, and found her dead, and, carrying her forth, buried her by her husband.*
v. 11, *And great fear came upon all the church, and upon as many as heard these things.*

1.   CHRISTIAN GENEROSITY

The early Church had a great love for one another and shared all things in common.

Acts 4:34-35, *Neither was there any among them that lacked: as many as were possessers of lands or houses sold them, and brought the prices of the things that were sold.*
v. 35, *And laid them down at the apostles' feet: and distribution was made unto every man according as he had need.*

A.   Every man's needs were supplied from a general fund.

B.   The supply for the distribution came from proceeds of the sale of property by the Church members.

2.   A SELFISH SCHEME TO SEEK PRAISE

Desiring the praise of men, a man and a woman lied about some of their income.

Acts 5:1-2, *But a certain man named Ananias, with Sapphira his wife, sold a possession,*
v. 2, And kept back part of the price, his wife also being privy to it, and brought a certain part, and laid it at the apostles' feet.

A.   Ananias and Sapphira appropriated part of the price for their own benefit.

B.   They hoped to get on the bandwagon for half-price.

C.   With a pious air, they laid a portion at the apostles' feet.

3.   SIN UNCOVERED

Through the gift of the Holy Spirit, the evil was supernaturally discerned.

Acts 5:3, *But Peter said, Ananias, why hath Satan filled thine heart to lie to the Holy Ghost, and to keep back a part of the price of the land?*

A.   The Holy Spirit detected the sin and turned on the searchlight.

B.   The Spirit gave Peter the right words to say.

C.   Hypocrisy could not exist in a Pentecostal atmosphere.

4.   SIN REBUKED

Without mincing words, Peter reprimanded the sinner.

Acts 5:4, *Whiles it remained, was it not thine own? and after it was sold, was it not in thine own power? why hast thou conceived this thing in thine heart? thou hast not lied unto men, but unto God.*

A.   The sin of Ananias was willful and inexcusable.

B.   He was under no obligation after it was sold.

C.   He told a deliberate lie in an attempt to deceive.

5. SIN PUNISHED

Ananias could not stand up against the truth.

Acts 5:5-6, *And Ananias hearing these words fell down, and gave up the ghost: and great fear came on all them that heard these things.*
v. 6, *And the young men arose, wound him up, and carried him out, and buried him.*

6. DIVINE JUDGMENT

A. Judgment must begin at the house of God.

I Peter 4:17, *For the time is come that judgment must begin at the house of God: and if it first begin at us, what shall the end be of them that obey not the gospel of God?*

B. Achan's death was an Old Testament example of the wrath of God. Because of one man's deed, God turned his back on Israel. Until the sin was punished, they cound not win any more battles with their enemies.

Joshua 7:11-12, 15, 20-21, 24-25, *Israel hath sinned, and they have transgressed my covenant which I commanded them: for they have even taken of the accursed thing, and have also stolen, and dissembled also, and they have put it even among their own stuff.*
v. 12, *Therefore the children of Israel could not stand before their enemies, but turned their backs before their enemies, because they were accursed: neither will I be with you any more, except ye destroy the accursed from among you.*

v. 15, *And it shall be, that he that is taken with the accursed thing shall be burnt with fire, he and all that he hath: because he hath transgressed the covenant of the LORD, and because he hath wrought folly in Israel.*

v. 20, *And Achan answered Joshua, and said, Indeed I have sinned against the LORD God of Israel, and thus and thus have I done.*
v. 21, *When I saw among the spoils a goodly Babylonish garment, and two hundred shekels of silver, and a wedge of gold of fifty shekels weight, then I coveted them, and took them; and, behold, they are hid in the earth in the midst of my tent, and the silver under it.*

v. 24, *And Joshua, and all Israel with him, took Achan the son of Zerah, and the silver, and the garment, and the wedge of gold, and his sons, and his daughters, and his oxen, and his asses, and his sheep, and his tent, and all that he had: and they brought them unto the valley of Achor.*

v. 25, *And Joshua said, Why hast thou troubled us? the LORD shall trouble thee this day. And all Israel stoned him with stones, and burned them with fire, after they had stoned them with stones.*

C. God wanted the early Church to know the penalty of sin.

Romans 6:23, *For the wages of sin is death; but the gift of God is eternal life through Jesus Christ our Lord.*

7. SAPPHIRA'S OPPORTUNITY

A. Sapphira entered expecting to share her husband's glory.

Acts 5:7, *And it was about the space of three hours after, when his wife, not knowing what was done, came in.*

B. Peter's question gave her the opportunity to confess and repent. However, equally guilty, she willfully lied. She also shared in the sudden punishment.

Acts 5:8-9, *And Peter answered unto her, Tell me whether ye sold the land for so much? And she said, Yea, for so much.*
v. 9, *Then Peter said unto her, How is it that ye have agreed together to tempt the Spirit of the Lord? behold, the feet of them which have buried thy husband are at the door, and shall carry thee out.*

8. RENEWED REVERENCE

The judgment of God effected a change in the people.

Acts 5:11, 13-14, *And great fear came upon all the church, and upon as many as heard these things.*

v. 13, *And of the rest durst no man join himself to them: but the people magnified them.*
v. 14, *And believers were the more added to the Lord, multitudes both of men and women.*

STUDY GUIDE

INDIANA CHRISTIAN UNIVERSITY

THE ACTS OF THE APOSTLES

Lesson 10

THE FIRST DIVINE DELIVERANCE

INTRODUCTION:

The atmosphere of holiness that had judged Ananias and Sapphira attracted the multitudes. The discerning of spirits revealed the reality of God and cleaned up the church. Bringing an end to lies and sin, this powerful endowment of the Spirit also brought an end of sickness and suffering, so that those over whom Peter's shadow passed were healed. However, the great influx of believers alarmed the Jewish leaders, stirring opposition and persecution.

READING:

Acts 5:11-15, *And great fear came upon all the church, and upon as many as heard these things.*
v. 12, *And by the hands of the apostles were many signs and wonders wrought among the people; (and they were all with one accord in Solomon's porch.*
v. 13, *And of the rest durst no man join himself to them: but the people magnified them.*
v. 14, *And believers were the more added to the Lord, multitudes both of men and women.)*
v. 15, *Insomuch that they brought forth the sick into the streets, and laid them on beds and couches, that at the least the shadow of Peter passing by might overshadow some of them.*

1.   THE INDIGNANT PRIEST

This wonderful demonstration of power was not well received by jealous religious leaders.

Acts 5:16-18, *There came also a multitude out of the cities round about unto Jerusalem, bring sick folks, and them which were vexed with unclean spirits: and they were healed every one.*
v. 17, *Then the high priest rose up and all they that were with him, (which is the sect of the saducees,) and were filled with indignation.*
v. 18, *And laid their hands on the apostles, and put them in the common prison.*

43

    A.   Envious priests and Sadducees caused the persecution.

    B.   They felt threatened by the power and influence of the Church.

    C.   The apostles had defied orders to keep silent about Jesus.

2. DIVINE DELIVERANCE

Supernaturally, the prisoners were released and ordered to resume witnessing in the Temple.

Acts 5:19-23, *But the angel of the Lord by night opened the prison doors, and brought them forth, and said,*
v. 20, *Go, stand and speak in the temple to the people all the words of this life.*
v. 21, *And when they heard that, they entered into the temple early in the morning, and taught. But the high priest came, and they that were with him, and called the council together, and all the senate of the children of Israel, and sent to the prison to have them brought.*
v. 22, *But when the officers came, and found them not in the prison, they returned, and told,*
v. 23, *Saying, The prison truly found we shut with all safety, and the keepers standing without before the doors: but when we had opened, we found no man within.*

    A.   This was the first, but not the last, divine deliverance in the early Church.

    B.   God sent an angel to open the prison doors.

    C.   God has control over both physical and spiritual forces.

3. THE PURPOSE

    A.   This divine deliverance freed the apostles to witness.

    B.   They were able to declare the life-giving action of the power of the Holy Ghost.

4. THE RESULTS

    A.   The apostles made an immediate return to the Temple.

    B.   At daybreak they began preaching the Gospel.

    C.   They could have run away, but their loyalty to God meant more.

    D.   They chose to obey God, rather than man.

    E.   The apostles were flogged and set free.

5.   APOSTLES RE-ARRESTED

Acts 5:24-26, *Now when the high priest and the captain of the temple and the chief priests heard these things, they doubted of them whereunto this would grow.*
v. 25, *Then came one and told them, saying, Behold, the men whom ye put in prison are standing in the temple, and teaching the people.*
v. 26, *Then went the captain with the officers, and brought them without violence: for they feared the people, lest they should have been stoned.*

    A.   The crowd was gathered for the apostles.

    B.   They could have easily caused a riot, but they made no resistance.

6.   ACCUSATION OF THE HIGH PRIEST

Acts 5:27-29, *And when they had brought them, they set them before the council: and the high priest asked them,*
v. 28, *Saying, Did not we straitly command you that ye should not teach in this name? and, behold, ye have filled Jerusalem with your doctrine, and intend to bring this man's blood upon us.*
v. 29, *Then Peter and the other apostles answered and said, We ought to obey God rather than men.*

    A.   The high priest accused the apostles of filling Jerusalem with their doctrine.

    B.   They were charged with spreading their teaching for the purpose of revenge.

    C.   The religious leaders realized that the believers were putting the responsibility for Jesus' death on them.

NOTES

STUDY GUIDE

INDIANA CHRISTIAN UNIVERSITY

THE ACTS OF THE APOSTLES

Lesson 11

THE FIRST CHURCH OFFICERS

INTRODUCTION:

After the persecution and deliverance described in the last lesson, we find that the Church kept growing, but all was not peace and contentment. We must not forget that an increase in numbers brings an increase in human responsibility problems. When these rough spots come, God's will for the believers is to keep filled with the Spirit.

READING:

Acts 6:3, *Wherefore, brethren, look ye out among you seven men of honest report, full of the Holy Ghost and wisdom, whom we may appoint over this business.*

1.   THERE WAS MURMURING AND DISCONTENT

At some time there was a quarrel between the Greek-speaking Jews and the native Jews.

Acts 6:1, *And in those days, when the number of the disciples was multiplied, there arose a murmuring of the Grecians against the Hebrews, because their widows were neglected in the daily ministration.*

A.   Certain widows were neglected.

B.   The multiplication of believers had increased responsibilities.

C.   It threatened spiritual unity.

2. ORGANIZATION WAS NEEDED

The apostles did not feel it was right for them to neglect their preaching to handle these problems.

Acts 6:2, *Then the twelve called the multitude of the disciples unto them, and said, It is not reason that we should leave the word of God, and serve tables.*

A. The apostles were sensitive to the Holy Spirit.

B. They called the people to consider the problem.

C. They could not leave their ministry to serve tables.

3. A WORD OF WISDOM

Acts 6:3-4, *Wherefore, brethren, look ye out among you seven men of honest report, full of the Holy Ghost and wisdom, whom we may appoint over this business.*
v. 4, *But we will give ourselves continually to prayer, and to the ministry of the word.*

A. Look for qualified men among you.

B. Make sure they are genuine, born-again believers.

C. They must be men of honest report.

D. See that they are full of the Holy Ghost.

E. They must be full of wisdom and ability.

4. APPOINTMENT OF DEACONS

Acts 6:5-6, *And the saying pleased the whole multitude: and they chose Stephen, a man full of faith and of the Holy Ghost, and Philip, and Prochorus, and Nicanor, and Timon, and Parmenas, and Nicolas a proselyte of Antioch:*
v. 6, *Whom they set before the apostles: and when they had prayed, they laid their hands on them.*

The apostles gave their full time to prayer and preaching. The whole group was pleased with the apostles' proposal; therefore, they chose seven men full of faith and the Holy Spirit to serve as deacons:

    A.   Stephen

    B.   Philip

    C.   Prochorus

    D.   Nicanor

    E.   Timon

    F.   Parmenas

    G.   Nicolas from Antioch, a Gentile converted to Judaism

5.   BLESSING INCREASED

Better organization helped the Church to spread the Gospel.

Acts 6:7, *And the word of God increased; and the number of the disciples multiplied in Jerusalem greatly; and a great company of the priests were obedient to the faith.*

    A.   The Word of God increased.

    B.   The number of disciples multiplied.

    C.   A great company of priests were obedient to the faith.

6.   GOD SET LEADERS IN THE CHURCH

Jesus Himself ordered the pattern of unity in the church.

Ephesians 4:11-13, *And he gave some, apostles; and some, prophets; and some, evangelists; and some, pastors and teachers;*
v. 12, *For the perfecting of the saints, for the work of the ministry, for the edifying of the body of Christ.*
v. 13, *Till we all come in the unity of the faith, and of the knowledge of the Son of God, unto a perfect man, unto the measure of the stature of the fulness of Christ.*

7.   THE HIGHEST CHURCH GOVERNOR WAS GOD

Although the apostles selected the elders who managed the churches, the final authority and supreme head of the Church was God.

Acts 14:23, *And when they had ordained them elders in every church, and had prayed with fasting, they commended them to the Lord, on whom they believed.*

A spiritual need arose in the Church. A condition developed which was carnal and was creating disunity and division. God was interested in this, for it threatened His Church and the Body of His Son. God's "watchmen," the apostles, took immediate note of the situation and guided the people by setting forth the qualifications of the men to be chosen. They reserved to themselves the actual official dedication to their work.

STUDY GUIDE

INDIANA CHRISTIAN UNIVERSITY

THE ACTS OF THE APOSTLES

Lesson 12

THE FIRST MARTYR FOR CHRIST

INTRODUCTION:

We have already seen how the apostles got into trouble because of their testimony for Christ. The early Church did not sit on the sidelines and let the apostles do all the work. They all witnessed, producing both results and reaction. When Stephen became a Spirit-filled believer, the evidence of God's favor ws overwhelming in faith, grace, and power. Yet this same man was willing to fulfill the humble task f being a deacon.

READING:

Acts 7:59, *And they stoned Stephen, calling upon God, and saying, Lord Jesus, receive my spirit.*

1. THE MINISTRY OF STEPHEN

    Richly blessed by God, Stephen was bold and obedient, reflecting the ministry of Jesus.

    Acts 6:8, *And Stephen, full of faith and power, did great wonders and miracles among the people.*

    A. He was full of faith and power of the Holy Spirit.

    B. Although Stephen was a deacon rather than a preacher, God used him to perform great wonders and miracles among the people.

    C. He proved the gifts of the Spirit were not just for the Day of Pentecost.

The First Martyr for Christ
Lesson 12

2. THE PLOT OF THE JEWS

Some Jews were angered by the functioning of the gifts of the Spirit through Stephen because it revealed their own lack of spiritual authority and power.

Acts 6:9-12, *Then there arose certain of the synagogue, which is called the synagogue of the Libertines, and Cyrenians, and Alexandrians, and of them of Cilicia and of Asia, disputing with Stephen.*
v. 10, And they were not able to resist the wisdom and the spirit by which he spake.
v. 11, Then they suborned men, which said, We have heard him speak blasphemous words against Moses, and against God.
v. 12, And they stirred up the people, and the elders, and the scribes, and came upon him, and caught him, and brought him to the council.

A. Stephen was invited to discuss the gospel in synagogues.

B. There the Holy Spirit shattered the arguments of the opponents.

C. They secured false witnesses to demonstrate against him.

D. Finally, they charged him with blasphemy against Moses.

3. SUDDEN ARREST

Acts 6:12, *And they stirred up the people, and the elders, and the scribes, and came upon him, and caught him, and brought him to the council.*

A. These men agitated the crowd that had gathered.

B. Stephen was dragged before the council.

4. A VICIOUS REACTION TO STEPHEN'S TESTIMONY

In the midst of this emotional furor, Stephen was granted a glimpse of heaven.

Acts 7:55-56, *But he, being full of the Holy Ghost, looked up stedfastly into heaven, and saw the glory of God, and Jesus standing on the right hand of God,*
v. 56, And said, Behold, I see the heavens opened, and the Son of man standing on the right hand of God.

A. Stephen was looking straight into heaven.

B. He saw God's glory and witnessed Jesus standing on the right hand of God.

52

5. THE DEATH OF A MARTYR

Unable to bear the words of Stephen, his accusers covered their ears with their hands and rushed forward to destroy him.

Acts 7:57-60, *They cried out with a loud voice, and stopped their ears, and ran upon him with one accord.*
v. 58, *And cast him out of the city, and stones him: and the witnesses laid down their clothes at a young man's feet, whose name was Saul.*
v. 59, *And they stoned Stephen, calling upon God, and saying, Lord Jesus, receive my spirit.*
v. 60, *And he kneeled down, and cried with a loud voice, Lord, lay not this sin to their charge. And when he had said this, he fell asleep.*

A. This testimony and vision were the climax of Stephen's witness.

B. He was cast out of the city and stoned.

C. He called upon God to receive his spirit.

D. He prayed that his persecutors be not charged for his death.

6. THE DEATH OF STEPHEN WAS NOT A DEFEAT

A young man who had probably also heard him preach, Saul of Tarsus, never forgot his experience. Saul later became Paul the apostle.

NOTES

_____

_____

_____

_____

_____

_____

_____

_____

_____

_____

_____

_____

_____

_____

_____

_____

_____

_____

_____

_____

_____

_____

_____

STUDY GUIDE

INDIANA CHRISTIAN UNIVERSITY

THE ACTS OF THE APOSTLES

Lesson 13

THE FIRST EVANGELISTIC MISSION

INTRODUCTION:

After the death of Stephen the entire Church in Jerusalem felt the fires of vicious persecution. As a result, the vast majority of believers fled from Jerusalem in every direction to become traveling evangelists. The persecution danger became a challenge-- there was no defeat in Jesus.

READING:

Acts 8:4-5, *Therefore they that were scattered abroad went every where preaching the word.*
v. 5, *Then Philip went down to the city of Samaria, and preached Christ unto them.*

1. PHILIP THE DEACON

A layman began the first recorded evangelistic mission of the Church. Through him the gifts of healings and miracles were functioning.

Acts 8:6-8, *And the people with one accord gave heed unto those things which Philip spake, hearing and seeing the miracles which he did.*
v. 7, *For unclean spirits, crying with loud voice, came out of many that were possessed with them: and many taken with palsies, and that were lame, were healed.*
v. 8, *And there was great joy in that city.*

A.   Philip went to Samaria and preached Christ. He was a fearless, obedient deacon.

B.   His message was accompanied by demonstrations of the Spirit and power.

C.   Demons departed, and the palsied, and lame were healed.

D.   Everywhere there was new-found joy.

2. THE MAGICIAN

Simon, a sorceror, deceived the Samaritans into regarding him with high esteem.

Acts 8:9-11, *But there was certain man, called Simon, which beforetime in the same city used sorcery, and bewitched the people of Samaria, giving out that himself was some great one:*
v. 10, *To whom they all gave heed, from the least to the greatest, saying, This man is the great power of God.*
v. 11, *And to him they had regard, because that of long time he had bewitched them with sorceries.*

A. A trickster named Simon used sorcery.

B. He had bewitched the people of Samaria for quite some time.

C. People from the lowest to the highest ranks of society greatly respected him and attended to what he said.

3. THE POWER OF GOD

After hearing the message about the name of Jesus and witnessing the powerful wonders which occurred through Philip's ministry, the people turned to God.

Acts 8:12-13, *But when they believed Philip preaching the things concerning the kingdom of God, and the name of Jesus Christ, they were baptized, both men and women.*
v. 13, *Then Simon himself believed also: and when he was baptized, he continued with Philip, and wondered, beholding the miracles and signs which were done.*

A. Philip preached the kingdom of God.

B. He glorified the name of Jesus.

C. Men and women were saved and baptized.

D. Simon believed and was baptized.

4. A PASTORAL VISIT

Acts 8:14, *Now when the apostles which were at Jerusalem heard that Samaria had received the word of God, they sent unto them Peter and John.*

A. The good news about salvation in Samaria traveled to the apostles in Jerusalem.

B. They were happy that Samaria had received the Word and sent preachers to the people.

5.   THE SPIRIT GIVEN

Acts 8:15-17, *Who, when they were come down, prayed for them, that they might receive the Holy Ghost:*
v. 16, *(For as yet he was fallen upon none of them: only they were baptized in the name of the Lord Jesus.)*
v. 17, *Then laid they their hands on them, and they received the Holy Ghost.*

A.   None of the Samaritans had received a personal baptism of the Holy Spirit.

B.   They needed power to strengthen, settle, and empower them.

C.   The apostles laid hands on them.

D.   They received the Holy Ghost.

6.   SIMON OFFERED MONEY FOR THE POWER

When Simon saw the miracles and healings occurring, he evidently did not understand the source from which they came. He had to be rebuked.

Acts 8:18-20, 24, *And when Simon saw that through laying on of the apostles hands the Holy Ghost was given, he offered them money.*
v. 19, *Saying, Give also this power, that on whomsoever I lay hands, he may receive the Holy Ghost.*
v. 20, *But Peter said unto him, Thy money perish with thee, because thou hast thought that the gift of God may be purchased with money.*
v. 24, *Then answered Simon, and said, Pray ye to the Lord for me, that none of these things which ye have spoken come upon me.*

A.   Peter reproved him.

B.   The reprimand humbled Simon, and he asked for prayer.

NOTES

STUDY GUIDE

INDIANA CHRISTIAN UNIVERSITY

THE ACTS OF THE APOSTLES

Lesson 14

THE GIFTS OF THE SPIRIT BRING JOY

INTRODUCTION:

The Church grew through the supernatural functions of the gifts of the Spirit. The infant Church did not grow because of its smooth organization. It did not increase because it had profound books to study. It did not expand due to its celebrated leaders. The early Church was a conquering church due to the operations of the gifts of the Spirit which brought joy to the people.

These nine gifts of the Spirit were so forceful that nothing could stand in their way. In chapters eight and nine of the Acts of the Apostles there are seven distinct performances of the gifts.

READING:

Acts 8:1, . . .*At that time there was a great persecution against the church which was at Jerusalem; and they were all scattered abroad throughout the regions of Judæa and Samaria, except the apostles.*

1. THE GIFTS OF THE SPIRIT WERE MANIFESTED
    A deacon from Jerusalem was led of the Lord to go to the city of Samaria, the capital of Syria, to preach. Miracles and healings abounded in his meetings.

    Acts 8:6-7, *And the people with one accord gave heed unto those things which Philip spake, hearing and seeing the miracles which he did.*
    v. 7, *For unclean spirits, crying with loud voice, came out of many that were possessed with them: and many taken with palsies, and that were lame, were healed.*

    A. Evil spirits were cast out by God's power. This was the gift of the working of miracles.

    B. The paralyzed and lame were healed.

59

2. A CITY REJOICED

Through this supernatural ministry of the gifts of the spirit, the people were filled with a new joy.

Acts 8:9, *And there was great joy in that city.*

3. WONDERS AND MIRACLES

The supernatural signs which attended Philip's ministry drew the attention of the local sorceror.

Acts 8:13, *Then Simon himself believed also: and when he was baptized, he continued with Philip, and wondered, beholding the miracles and signs which were done.*

These were also the gifts of healing and the working of miracles.

4. MORE MIRACLES

A. Philip went down to the desert where he found an Ethiopian studying the scriptures. Finding that the man did not understand what he was reading, Philip joined him and   taught him about the Lord Jesus Christ. Immediately, the man desired to be baptized. When they came out of the water, another miracle occured.

Acts 8:39-40, *And when they were come up out of the water, the Spirit of the Lord caught away Philip, that the eunuch saw him no more: and he went on his way rejoicing.*
v. 40, *But Philip was found at Azotus: and passing through he preached in all the cities, till he came to Cæsarea.*

1) Those who have worked around heathenism and spiritism know that people who believe in demon power think that they can be transported from one place to another immediately through demon power.

2) We find that in the working of the gifts of the Spirit such a phenomena is possible. Philip was transported 20 to 30 miles away.

3) The devil always tries to produce a counterfeit of God's reality.

B.   Saul experienced a miracle on the road to Damascus.

Acts 9:3-5, *And as he journeyed, he came near Damascus: and suddenly there shined round about him a light from heaven:*
v. 4, And he fell to the earth, and heard a voice saying unto him, Saul, Saul, why persecutest thou me?
v. 5, And he said, Who art thou Lord? And the Lord said, I am Jesus whom thou persecutest: it is hard for thee to kick against the pricks.

1)   An unnatural light shone from the sky with such intensity that it blinded Paul.

2)   A divine voice resounded.

5.   GIFT OF THE WORD OF WISDOM

The word of wisdom operated through Jesus in that He supernaturally knew the future. He was able to foretell what would happen to Saul.

Acts 9:6, *And he trembling and astonished said, Lord, what wilt thou have me to do? And the Lord said unto him, Arise, and go into the city, and it shall be told thee what thou must do.*

6.   GIFT OF THE WORD OF KNOWLEDGE

A word of knowledge came to Ananias that a man named Saul was praying.

Acts 9:17-19, *And Ananias went his way, and entered into the house; and putting his hands on him said, Brother Saul, the Lord, even Jesus, that appeared unto thee in the way as thou camest, hath sent me, that thou mightest receive thy sight, and be filled with the Holy Ghost.*
v. 18, And immediately there fell from his eyes as it had been scales: and he received sight forthwith, and arose, and was baptized.
v. 19, And when he had received meat, he was strengthened. Then was Saul certain days with the disciples which were at Damascus.

A.   Because of the word of knowledge when Ananias reached Saul, he already knew that God had appeared to him.

B.   This gift of the Spirit told Ananias where to find Saul, and what to do when he reached him.

C.   Saul was supernaturally healed of blindness.

7.   GIFTS OF HEALING

The functioning of the gifts of healing resulted in marvelous revival. The gifts of the Spirit bring with them a movement of conviction that draws people to the Lord Jesus Christ.

A.   Aeneas had been paralyzed for years, but was instantly healed by one of the gifts of the Spirit. Everyone in the vicinity turned to the Lord.

Acts 9:32-35, *And it came to pass, as Peter passed throughout all quarters, he came down also to the saints which dwelt at Lydda.*
v. 33, And there he found a certain man named Aeneas, which had kept his bed eight years, and was sick of the palsy.
v. 34, And Peter said unto him, Aeneas, Jesus Christ maketh thee whole: arise, and make thy bed. And he arose immediately.
v. 35, And all that dwelt at Lydda and Saron saw him, and turned to the Lord.

B.   Dorcas, a woman full of good works, received a miraculous healing.

Acts 9:39-42, *Then Peter arose and went with them. When he was come, they brought him into the upper chamber: and all the widows stood by him weeping, and shewing the coats and garments which Dorcas made, while she was with them.*
v. 40, But Peter put them all forth, and kneeled down, and prayed; and turning him to the body said, Tabitha, arise. And she opened her eyes: and when she saw Peter, she sat up.
v. 41, And he gave her his hand, and lifted her up, and when he had called the saints and widows, presented her alive.
v. 42, And it was known throughout all Joppa; and many believed in the Lord.

1)   Peter put sentiment out of the room. He moved all the mourners to another place.

2)   He called the body of the woman by name, telling her to arise.

3)   He presented her alive to the widows and saints.

4)   When the miracle of healing took place, the people believed in God.

STUDY GUIDE

INDIANA CHRISTIAN UNIVERSITY

THE ACTS OF THE APOSTLES

Lesson 15

THE FIRST MISSIONARY CONVERT

INTRODUCTION:

After the great city-wide revival in Samaria, an angel appeared unto Philip with a message from the Lord. He was told to leave the crowds behind and go into the desert.

READING:

Acts 8:27, *And he arose and went: and, behold a man of Ethiopia, an eunuch of great authority under Candace queen of the Ethiopians, who had the charge of all her treasure, and had come to Jerusalem for to worship.*

1.   A STRANGE COMMAND

An angel told Philip to leave Samaria.

Acts 8:26, *And the angel of the Lord spake unto Philip, saying, Arise, and go toward the south unto the way that goeth down from Jerusalem unto Gaza, which is desert.*

A.   Philip did not question the unusual order.

B.   He arose and traveled to the designated place.

C.   An Ethiopian rode leisurely toward Africa.

D.   This eunuch was a high-ranking government official under Queen Candace.

E.   He had come to Jerusalem to worship and was returning home.

2. GOD-GIVEN OPPORTUNITY

Unknown to Philip, this man trusted by the queen, was seeking knowledge of God by studying the scriptures.

Acts 8:27-30, . . .*a man of Ethiopia. . .*
v. 28, *Was returning, and sitting in his chariot read Esaias the prophet.*
v. 29, *Then the Spirit said unto Philip, Go near, and join thyself to this chariot.*
v. 30, *And Philip ran thither to him, and heard him read the prophet Esaias, and said, Understandest thou what thou readest?*

A. While sitting in his chariot, the Ethiopian was reading from Isaiah, the prophet.

B. A spiritual hunger after God had taken him to Jerusalem.

C. The Spirit sent Philip to join himself to the chariot.

D. As an obedient witness, Philip ran to him.

E. Hearing him read, Philip asked if he understood.

3. A PERPLEXING PASSAGE

The passage was confusing, and the frustrated man invited Philip to sit with him and discuss it.

Acts 8:31-35, *And he said, How can I, except some man should guide me? And he desired Philip that he would come up and sit with him.*
v. 32, *The place of the scripture which he read ws this, He was led as a sheep to the slaughter; and like a lamb dumb before his shearer, so opened he not his mouth:*
v. 33, *In his humiliation his judgment was taken away: and who shall declare his generation? for his life is taken from the earth.*
v. 34, *And the eunuch answered Philip, and said, I pray thee, of whom speaketh the prophet this? of himself, or of some other man?*
v. 35, *Then Philip opened his mouth, and began at the same scripture, and preached unto him Jesus.*

A. The eunuch asked, "How can I understand except some man guide me?"

B. He urged Philip to climb into the chariot.

C. The eunuch was reading the 53rd chapter of Isaiah.

D. He questioned, "Is the prophet speaking of himself or another?"

E. Philip, recognizing the passage, preached Jesus to the man.

4.   A SATISFIED HEART AND MIND

Eagerly the eunuch listened to the message of Jesus told by the missionary.

Acts 8:36-39, *And as they went on their way, they came unto a certain water: and the eunuch said, See, here is water; what doth hinder me to be baptized?*
v. 37, *And Philip said, If thou believest with all thine heart, thou mayest. And he answered and   said, I believe that Jesus Christ is the Son of God.*
v. 38, *And he commanded the chariot to stand still: and they went down both into the water, both Philip and the eunuch; and he baptized him.*
v. 39, *And when they were come up out of the water, the Spirit of the Lord caught away Philip, that the eunuch saw him no more: and he went on his way rejoicing.*

A.   As they were riding, they passed a pool of water.

B.   The eunuch's desire to be baptized indicated his new faith.

C.   Philip and the eunuch both went down into the water.

D.   When they came up, the Spirit caught Philip away.

E.   The eunuch went on his way rejoicing.

NOTES

STUDY GUIDE

INDIANA CHRISTIAN UNIVERSITY

THE ACTS OF THE APOSTLES

Lesson 16

THE FIRST PERSECUTOR CONVERTED

INTRODUCTION:

This event is one of the highlights of the book. Here the chief opponent of the gospel becomes its chief proponent.

READING:

Acts 26:14-16, *And when we were all fallen to the earth, I heard a voice speaking unto me, and saying in the Hebrew tongue, Saul, Saul, why persecutest thou me? it is hard for thee to kick against the pricks.*
v. 15, *And I said, Who art thou, Lord? And he said, I am Jesus whom thou persecutest.*
v. 16, *But arise, and stand upon thy feet: for I have appeared unto thee for this purpose, to make thee a minister and a witness both of these things which thou hast seen, and of those things in the which I will appear unto thee.*

1.   SAUL'S MISTAKE

Mentally, Saul was convinced that he ws performing God's will.

Acts 26:9, *I verily thought within myself, that I ought to do many things contrary to the name of Jesus of Nazareth.*

A.   His murderous intentions were against God, not man.

B.   An atmosphere of hate controlled him.

2.   A MISDIRECTED ZEAL

Saul zealously pursued men and women who believed in Jesus, binding them, imprisoning them, and seeking their deaths.

67

Acts 9:1-2, *And Saul, yet breathing out threatenings and slaughter against the disciples of the Lord, went unto the high priest,*
v. 2, *And desired of him letters to Damascus to the synagogues, that if he found any of this way, whether they were men or women, he might bring them bound unto Jerusalem.*

A.   Relentlessly Saul harassed and tormented the disciples.

B.   He received letters from the high priest authorizing him to go to Damascus.

C.   He wanted to further persecute them and bring them back to Jerusalem for punishment.

3.   SAUL'S REVELATION

As he traveled toward Damascus, the God whom Saul was persecuting suddenly revealed Himself.

Acts 9:3-5, *And as he journeyed, he came near Damascus: and suddenly there shined round about him a light from heaven:*
v. 4, *And he fell to the earth, and heard a voice saying unto him, Saul, Saul, why persecutest thou me?*
v. 5, *And he said, Who art thou, Lord? And the Lord said, I am Jesus whom thou persecutest: it is hard for thee to kick against the pricks.*

A.   As they journeyed, they saw an unexpected light.

B.   It was brighter than the noonday sun.

C.   Falling to the ground, Saul heard a voice of warning.

4.   A NEW BELIEVER

His murderous intentions were erased as heaven's light filled Saul's darkened mind and soul.

Acts 9:6, *And he trembling and astonished said, Lord, what wilt thou have me to do? And the Lord said unto him, Arise, and go into the city, and it shall be told thee what thou must do.*

A.   Shaking with amazement, Saul asked, "Who art thou?"

B.   He cried, "What will you have me to do?"

5.   A HUMBLED BELIEVER

Obeying the voice of the Lord, Saul, now helpless, continued toward Damascus.

Acts 9:8-9,And Saul arose from the earth; and when his eyes were opened, he saw no man: but they led him by the hand, and brought him into Damascus.
v. 9, And he was three days without sight, and neither did eat nor drink.

A.   He arose and went on in to Damascus.

B.   There he spent three days in fasting and blindness.

6.   A PRAYING BELIEVER

A.   While he was praying, Paul received a vision which assured him that his blindness was temporary.

Acts 9:12, And (Saul) hath seen in a vision a man named Ananias coming in, and putting his hand on him, that he might receive his sight.

B.   God also spoke in a vision to Ananias concerning Saul, the new believer.

Acts 9:10, And there was a certain disciple at Damascus, named Ananias; and to him said the Lord in a vision, Ananias. And he said, Behold, I am here, Lord.

C.   God hears the prayers of His children. He sent a word of knowledge to Ananias with specific directions to find Saul.

Acts 9:11, And the Lord said unto him, Arise, and go into the street which is called Straight, and inquire in the house of Judas for one called Saul, of Tarsus: for, behold, he prayeth.

D.   Ananias felt compelled to remind God that Saul was a dangerous enemy whose reputation had preceded him

Acts 9:13-14, Then Ananias answered, Lord, I have heard by many of this man, how much evil he hath done to thy saints at Jerusalem:
v. 14, And here he hath authority from the chief priests to bind all that call on thy name.

E.   God revealed that he had chosen Saul to be a witness before the gentiles, kings, and the Jews.

Acts 9:15-16, *But the Lord said unto him, Go thy way: for he is a chosen vessel unto me, to bear my name before the Gentiles, and kings, and the children of Israel:*
v. 16, *For I will shew him how great things he must suffer for my name's sake.*

7.   A SATISFIED BELIEVER

Following God's detailed instructions, Ananias boldly introduced himself to the man who had been the Christians' worst oppressor.

Acts 9:17-18, *And Ananias went his way, and entered into the house; and putting his hands on him said, Brother Saul, the Lord, even Jesus, that appeared unto thee in the way as thou camest, hath sent me, that thou mightest receive thy sight, and be filled with the Holy Ghost.*
v. 18, *And immediately there fell from his eyes as it had been scales: and he received sight forthwith, and arose, and was baptized.*

A.   Ananias came under divine direction.

B.   In Christian love, he called his former enemy, "Brother Saul."

C.   He prayed, and the scales fell from Saul's eyes.

D.   Saul arose and was baptized.

8.   AN ENTHUSIASTIC BELIEVER

The new convert did not hesitate to preach Christ.

Acts 9:20-22, *And straightway he preached Christ in the synagogues, that he is the Son of God.*
v. 21, *But all that heard him were amazed, and said; Is not this he that destroyed them which called on this name in Jerusalem, and came hither for that intent, that he might bring them bound unto the chief priests?*
v. 22, *But Saul increased the more in strength, and confounded the Jews which dwelt at Damascus, proving that this is very Christ.*

A.   Saul increased in strength.

B.   The Jews at Damascus were confounded.

STUDY GUIDE

INDIANA CHRISTIAN UNIVERSITY

THE ACTS OF THE APOSTLES

Lesson 17

THE CHURCH ATTACKS NATIONALISM

INTRODUCTION:

This lesson is very important. It demonstrates that the gifts of the Spirit jumped over national barriers and cultural roadblocks. No lines can be drawn, whether by wealth, culture, social status, education, or race. The Body of Christ is composed of anyone who will believe upon the Lord Jesus Christ and be saved, and we must keep it that way. The Church must destroy nationalism.

READING:

Acts 10:15, *And the voice spake unto him again the second time, What God hath cleansed, that call not thou common.*

1. THE GIFT OF THE WORD OF KNOWLEDGE WAS GIVEN TO CORNELIUS

    A. A rich Roman officer named Cornelius was living in Cæsarea, a seaport named after the Emperor, or Cæsar, of Rome. This man was the commander of at least 100 Roman soldiers, but he honored the God of the Jews.

    Acts 10:1-2, *There was a certain man in Cæsarea called Cornelius, a centurion of the band called the Italian band.*
    v. 2, A devout man, and one that feared God with all his house, which gave much alms to the people, and prayed to God alway.

    B. At about three o'clock in the afternoon Cornelius received a tremendous word of knowledge through an angel. God recognizes the prayers and offerings that are presented to him.

    Acts 10:3-4, *He saw in a vision evidently about the ninth hour of the day an angel of God coming in to him, and saying unto him, Cornelius.*

v. 4, *And when he looked on him, he was afraid, and said, What is it Lord? And he said unto him, Thy prayers and thine alms are come up for a memorial before God.*

C. He was given complete directions for finding a man named Simon Peter, who could tell Cornelius what he needed to know.

Acts 10:5-6, *And now end men to Joppa, and call for one Simon, whose surname is Peter:*
v. 6, *He lodgeth with one Simon a tanner, whose house is by the sea side: he shall tell thee what thou oughtest to do.*

1) It was revealed to Cornelius what city Peter was in at that moment. Peter was staying in Joppa, near Tel Aviv, about 100 miles south of Cæsarea.

2) He was also told Peter's entire name: Simon Peter.

3) The name of Peter's host was disclosed: Simon.

4) The host was identified as a tanner.

5) Simon's house was indicated as being by the seaside.

D. Immediately Cornelius sent his most trusted men to Joppa.

Acts 10:7-8, *And when the angel which spake unto Cornelius was departed, he called two of his household servants, and a devout soldier of them that waited on him continually;*
v. 8, *And when he had declared all these things unto them, he sent them to Joppa.*

2. A WORD OF KNOWLEDGE WAS ALSO GIVEN TO PETER

The other half of this miracle begins with verse nine. Peter was a Jew, and Cornelius was a Roman. They had nothing in common. Peter was under the subjection of Rome. Therefore Cornelius represented a type of tyranny to Peter. Besides, as far as Peter was concerned, Cornelius was pagan. God had to break down this barrier for the Church to be great.

A. Peter was on the housetop praying about noon.

Acts 10:9, *On the morrow, as they went on their journey, and drew nigh unto the city, Peter went up upon the housetop to pray about the sixth hour.*

    B.   There he saw a vision from God.

        Acts 10:10, *And he became very hungry, and would have eaten: but while they made ready, he fell into a trance.*

    C.   Peter saw heaven opened and a great sheet descending.

        Acts 10:11, *And saw heaven opened, and a certain vessel descending unto him, as it had been a great sheet knit at the four corners, and let down to the earth.*

    D.   All kinds of four-footed animals, creeping things, and fowls were in that sheet.

        Acts 10:12, *Wherein were all manner of fourfooted beasts of the earth, and wild beasts, and creeping things, and fowls of the air.*

    E.   God spoke in an audible voice, "Rise. Kill. Eat."

        Acts 10:13, *And there came a voice to him, Rise, Peter; kill, and eat.*

    F.   When he was commanded to eat, Peter absolutely refused. He replied, "No, Lord. I never eat that which is common or unclean." He tried to argue with the Lord.

        Acts 10:14, *But Peter said, Not so, Lord; for I have never eaten any thing that is common or unclean.*

    G.   Personal habit, opinion, or prejudice hinders God. The Lord responded, "Do not call unclean what God has cleansed."

        Acts 10:15, *And the voice spake unto him again the second time, What God hath cleansed, that call not thou common.*

    H.   Three times his prejudice was rebuked.

        Acts 10:16, *This was done thrice: and the vessel was received up again into heaven.*

4.   THE SPIRIT'S COMMAND

    A.   Three men sent from Cæsarea arrived at the house where Peter was staying.

Acts 10:17-18, *Now while Peter doubted in himself what this vision which he had seen should mean, behold, the men which were sent from Cornelius had made inquiry for Simon's house, and stood before the gate.*
v. 18, And called, and asked whether Simon, which was surnamed Peter, were lodged there.

B. The Spirit of the Lord announced the arrival of the men to Peter and ordered him to go with them without doubting.

Acts 10:19-20, *While Peter thought on the vision, the Spirit said unto him, Behold, three men seek thee.*
v. 20, Arise therefore, and get thee down, and go with them, doubting nothing: for I have sent them.

C. Although the example in the vision pertained to food, Peter realized the principle could be applied to men. To Peter's Old Testament training, a gentile home was unclean, and it was not proper to visit such a place. Now God was removing this restraint.

Acts 10:28, *And he said unto them, Ye know how that it is an unlawful thing for a man that is a Jew to keep company, or come unto one of another nation; but God hath shewed me that I should not call any man common or unclean.*

D. He went with the men to Cornelius' house, taking several brethren to witness God's work.

Acts 10 23, *. . .And on the morrow Peter went away with them, and certain brethren from Joppa accompanied him.*

E. Upon his return, he met with criticism.

Acts 11:1-3, *And the apostles and brethren that were in Judæa heard that the Gentiles had also received the word of God.*
v. 2, And when Peter was come up to Jerusalem, they that were of the circumcision contended with him.
v. 3, Saying, Thou wentest in to men uncircumcised, and didst eat with them.

4. AN ANGELIC CONFIRMATION

A. God had prepared the way in Cæsarea by His angel.

B. Peter's vision applied to the household of Cornelius.

C. Peter did not argue with the men or allow prejudice to hold him back.

D. Without hesitation, he declared that God shows no partiality.

5. THE GENTILES ACCEPT

A. Peter preached the Word to the Gentiles gathered at the home of Cornelius.

1) First he acknowledged that God must be making salvation available to everyone, regardless of nationality.

Acts 10:34-35, *Then Peter opened his mouth, and said, Of a truth I perceive that God is no respecter of persons:*
v. 35, But in every nation he that feareth him, and worketh righteousness, is accepted with him.

2) Next he witnessed of Jesus, explaining how sins could be forgiven.

Acts 10:38-40, 43, *How God anointed Jesus of Nazareth with the Holy Ghost and with power: who went about doing good, and healing all that were oppressed of the devil; for God was with him.*
v. 39, And we are witnesses of all things which he did both in the land of the Jews, and in Jerusalem; whom they slew and hanged on a tree:
v. 40, Him God raised up the third day, and shewed him openly;
v. 43, To him give all the prophets witness, that through his name whosoever believeth in him shall receive remission of sins.

B. The result was Pentecost.

Acts 10:44, *While Peter yet spake these words, the Holy Ghost fell on all them which heard the word.*

C. The convincing evidence was that they heard them speaking in tongues.

Acts 10:45-46, *And they of the circumcision which believed were astonished, as many as came with Peter, because that on the Gentiles also was poured out the gift of the Holy Ghost.*
v. 46, For they heard them speak with tongues, and magnify God.

D. He allowed them to declare their faith by water baptism.

Acts 10:47-48, *Can any man forbid water that these should not be baptized, which have received the Holy Ghost as well as we?*
v. 48, And he commanded them to be baptized in the name of the Lord. Then prayed they him to tarry certain days.

E. Peter's critics had to forget their prejudice and fence-building.

Acts 11:18, *When they heard these things, they held their peace, and glorified God, saying, Then hath God also to the Gentiles granted repentance unto life.*

NOTES

_____
_____
_____
_____
_____
_____
_____
_____
_____
_____
_____
_____
_____
_____
_____
_____
_____
_____
_____
_____
_____
_____
_____
_____
_____

STUDY GUIDE

INDIANA CHRISTIAN UNIVERSITY

THE ACTS OF THE APOSTLES

Lesson 18

THE FIRST MISSIONARY CHURCH

INTRODUCTION:

The early Christians had burning hearts. They became lights in the midst of a darkened world.

READING:

Acts 11:20, *And some of them were men of Cyprus and Cyrene, which when they were come to Antioch, spake unto the Grecians, preaching the Lord Jesus.*

1. TRAVELING WITNESSES

    Rather than cower in fear, the Christians who were forced to flee from Jerusalem proclaimed their faith to the Jews they met.

    Acts 11:19, *Now they which were scattered abroad upon the persecution that arose about Stephen travelled as fas as Phenice, and Cyprus, and Antioch, preaching the word to none but unto the Jews only.*

    A.   Tests and trials did not destroy the Church.

    B.   Satan hoped to diminish them, but they moved in every direction.

    C.   Persecution spurred them on to greater things.

    D.   They talked about Jesus everywhere.

2.   ENTERING NEW TERRITORY

Unable to contain the fire of God's Spirit that was burning within them, some nameless men of Cyprus and Cyrene obeyed the Holy Spirit and began preaching Jesus to the Greeks.

Acts 11:20, *And some of them were men of Cyprus and Cyrene, which, when they were come to Antioch, spake unto the Grecians, preaching the Lord Jesus.*

A.   Their lives had been limited to the Jews only.

B.   The fire got so hot they could not hold it in.

C.   The Holy Spirit directed them to preach to the Gentiles.

D.   Some people limit the Holy Spirit to ruts they created.

3.   REVIVAL IN ANTIOCH

One does not need a particular office or gift to preach the Gospel. Just believe, and the signs will follow.

Acts 11:21, *And the hand of the Lord was with them: and a great number believed, and turned unto the Lord.*

A.   God did miracles on behalf of their simple witness.

B.   The hand of the Lord was with them.

C.   A great number believed and turned to the Lord.

4.   ENCOURAGEMENT FROM JERUSALEM

The Church at Jerusalem heard the news and sent Barnabas to minister to them.

Acts 11:22-24, *Then tidings of these things came unto the ears of the church which was in Jerusalem: and they sent forth Barnabas, that he should go as far as Antioch.*
v. 23, *Who, when he came, and had seen the grace of God, was glad, and exhorted them all, that with purpose of heart they would cleave unto the Lord.*
v. 24, *For he was a good man, and full of the Holy Ghost and of faith: and much people was added unto the Lord.*

A.   Desiring the new converts to receive full benefits of the Gospel, Barnabas encouraged them to abide in the Lord.

B.   Under the leadership of Barnabas, more new converts were added to the Church.

5.   A CHURCH ESTABLISHED

The Church grew in Antioch and Barnabas needed help.

Acts 11:25-26, *Then departed Barnabas to Tarsus, for to seek Saul:*
v. 26, *And when he had found him, he brought him unto Antioch. And it came to pass, that a whole year they assembled themselves with the church, and taught much people. And the disciples were called Christians first in Antioch.*

A.   He obeyed the Spirit and brought the Apostle Paul to teach the new converts.

B.   Paul assisted Barnabas for a whole year.

C.   The Church continued to be a thriving missionary center.

D.   The fires of revival kept burning due to daily public gatherings.

6.   THE DISCIPLES WERE CALLED CHRISTIANS

The city noticed there was something different about the disciples.

Acts 11:26. . .*And the disciples were called Christians first in Antioch.*

A.   The people of Antioch nicknamed them Christians.

B.   They were loyal, diligent followers of Christ.

NOTES

STUDY GUIDE

INDIANA CHRISTIAN UNIVERSITY

THE ACTS OF THE APOSTLES

Lesson 19

THE CHURCH IN THE STORM

INTRODUCTION:

Those who live godly lives will suffer persecution, and where the gifts of the Spirit are operating, the devil will stir up trouble. The gifts in operation in Acts chapters 12 and 13 are the gifts of power: the gift of faith and the gift of the working of miracles. The gift of working of miracles is when God does something through you. The gift of faith is when God does something for you.

READING:

Acts 12:1-3, *Now about that time Herod the king stretched forth his hands to vex certain of the church.*
v. 2, *And he killed James the brother of John with the sword.*
v. 3, *And because he saw it pleased the Jews, he proceeded further to take Peter also. (Then were the days of unleavened bread.)*

1. THE GIFT OF FAITH

    In chapter 12 the gift of faith was manifested when an angel rescued Peter.

    A. Acts 12:6-7, *And when Herod would have brought him forth, the same night Peter was sleeping between two soldiers, bound with two chains: and the keepers before the door kept the prison.*
        v. 7, *And, behold, the angel of the Lord came upon him, and a light shined in the prison: and he smote Peter on the side, and raised him up, saying, Arise up quickly. And his chains fell off from his hands.*

        1) An angel walked through doors and walls as Jesus did after His resurrection.

        2) The chains fell off Peter. There was no breaking, nor noise, nor key.

81

B. The iron gate opened of itself, and Peter walked free into the streets of Jerusalem.

Acts 12:10, *When they were past the first and the second ward, they came unto the iron gate that leadeth unto the city; which opened to them of his own accord: and they went out, and passed on through one street; and forthwith the angel departed from him.*

C. Finally comprehending that God had set him free, Peter shared the news with other believers before he left the city.

Acts 12:11-12, *And when Peter was come to himself, he said, Now I know of a surety, that the Lord hath sent his angel, and hath delivered me out of the hand of Herod, and from all the expectation of the people of the Jews.*
v. 12, *And when he had considered the thing, he came to the house of Mary the mother of John, whose surname was Mark; where many were gathered together praying.*

A. Peter came to the home of Mary, the mother of John.

B. The whole Church rejoiced.

2. THE GIFT OF THE WORKING OF MIRACLES

A. God called two men to a special work and used them to manifest a miracle.

Acts 13:1-2, *Now there were in the church that was at Antioch certain prophets and teachers; as Barnabas, and Simeon that was called Niger, and Lucius of Cyrene, and Manaen, which had been brought up with Herod the tetrarch, and Saul.*
v. 2, *As they ministered to the Lord, and fasted, the Holy Ghost said, Separate me Barnabas and Saul for the work whereunto I have called them.*

B. Directed by the Holy Ghost, the men preached the Word of God to the Jews at Salamis.

Acts 13:5, *And when they were at Salamis, they preached the word of God in the synagogues of the Jews: and they had also John to their minister.*

C. On the island of Cyprus a false prophet named Bar-jesus tried to hinder the work.

Acts 13:6-8, *And when they had gone through the isle unto Paphos, they found a certain sorcerer, a false prophet, a Jew, whose name was Bar-jesus:*
v. 7, Which was with the deputy of the country, Sergius Paulus, a prudent man; who called for Barnabas and Saul, and desired to hear the word of God.
v. 8, But Elymas the sorcerer (for so is his name by interpretation) withstood them, seeking to turn away the deputy from the faith.

D. Paul commanded him to go blind because of his wickedness in turning people away from God.

Acts 13:9-11, *Then Saul, (who also is called Paul,) filled with the Holy Ghost, set his eyes on him,*
v. 10, And said, O full of all subtilty and all mischief, thou child of the devil, thou enemy of all righteousness, wilt thou not cease to pervert the right ways of the Lord?
v. 11, And now, behold, the hand of the Lord is upon thee, and thou shalt be blind, not seeing the sun for a season. And immediately there fell on him a mist and a darkness; and he went about seeking some to lead him by the hand.

This performance of the gift of working of miracles was a sign to the unbelievers. It proved that the God Paul served was mightier than the sorcery of Bar-jesus.

NOTES

STUDY GUIDE

INDIANA CHRISTIAN UNIVERSITY

THE ACTS OF THE APOSTLES

Lesson 20

THE CHURCH DISCOVERS THE FICKLENESS OF HUMAN NATURE

INTRODUCTION:

When politics and religion get together, God's servants are in trouble because human nature changes and popular opinion wavers. In Acts 14 the gifts of the Spirit were manifested, thrilling the populace. However, the people rejected God, and readily turned against the apostles.

READING:

Acts 14:1-2, *And it came to pass in Iconium, that they went both together into the synagogue of the Jews, and so spake, that a great multitude both of the Jews and also of the Greeks believed.*
v. 2, *But the unbelieving Jew stirred up the Gentiles, and made their minds evil affected against the brethren.*

1. THE GIFTS OF THE SPIRIT OPERATED THROUGH PAUL AND BARNABAS

    A. They spoke boldly for Christ.

        Acts 14:3, *Long time therefore abode they speaking boldly in the Lord...*

    B. They proved their message:

        1) by signs

            Acts 14:3, *...which gave testimony unto the word of his grace, and granted signs and wonders to be done by their hands.*

     2)   by wonders

          Acts 14:3, . . .and wonders. . .

     3)   by miracles

          Acts 14:19-20, *And there came thither certain Jews from Antioc and Iconium, who persuaded the people, and, having stones Paul, drew him out of the city, supposing he had been dead.*
          v. 20, Howbeit, as the disciples stood round about him, he rose up, and came into the city: and the next day he departed with Barnabas to Derbe.

     4)   by healings

          Acts 14:8-10, *And there sat a certain man at Lystra, impotent in his feet, being a cripple from his mother's womb, who never had walked:*
          v. 9, The same heard Paul speak: who stedfastly beholding him, and perceiving that he had faith to be healed,
          v. 10, Said with a loud voice, Stand upright on thy feet. And he leaped and walked.

     5)   by supernatural revelation

          Acts 14:5-6, *And when there was an assault made both of the Gentiles, and also of the Jews with their rulers, to use them despitefully, and to stone them,*
          v. 6, They were ware of it, and fled unto Lystra and Derbe, cities of Lycaonia, and unto the region that lieth round about.

C.   Three gifts of the Spirit were indicated in this list:

     1)   The gift of the working of miracles includes three functions:

          a)   signs
          b)   miracles
          c)   wonders

     2)   The gifts of healing operated, and a lame man walked.

     3)   The word of wisdom supernaturally revealed the plan of the Jews to the apostles.

D.   In Iconia the people refused the evidence of God's power.

     Acts 14:4, *But the multitude of the city was divided: and part held with the Jews, and part with the apostles.*

E.   They sought to destroy the servants of God (Acts 14:5).

2.   THE GIFTS OF HEALING IN OPERATION AT LYSTRA

The apostles left Iconia and came to Lystra where they found a lame man, crippled from birth (Acts 14:8-10).

A.   The man had never walked.

B.   Paul witnessed to his faith.

C.   Paul commanded him to stand up and walk.

D.   The man jumped up and started walking around.

3.   HUMAN FICKLENESS

A.   The people had the wrong attitude. They wanted to make gods of the messengers of God. This is still a true tendency even today.

Acts 14:11, 18, *And when the people saw what Paul had done they lifted up their voices, saying in the speech of Lycaonia, The gods are come down to us in the likeness of men.*
v. 18, . . .scarce restrained they the people, that they had not done sacrifice unto them.

B.   These same people later stoned Paul and dragged him out of town, thinking he was dead.

Acts 14:19, *And there came thither certain Jews from Antioch and Iconium, who persuaded the people, and, having stoned Paul, drew him out of the city, supposing he had been dead.*

4.   THE GIFT OF THE WORKING OF MIRACLES

Paul was raised from the dead. Acts 14:20 records that as the disciples gathered around him, he stood up and walked back into the city.

NOTES

STUDY GUIDE

INDIANA CHRISTIAN UNIVERSITY

THE ACTS OF THE APOSTLES

Lesson 21

THE FIRST CHURCH COUNCIL

INTRODUCTION:

Chapter 15 deals with a Church problem. The Judæans tried to bring the newborn Church under the laws of Moses. Then two apostles quarreled. Often the gifts of the Spirit cannot function or operate because the Church is involved with carnal activities or dealing with legalism. The Church must flow in the Spirit for the gifts to operate.

READING:

Acts 15:1-2, *And certain men which came down from Judæa taught the brethren, and said, Except ye be circumcised after the manner of Moses, ye cannot be saved.*
v. 2, *When therefore Paul and Barnabas had no small dissension and disputation with them, they determined that Paul and Barnabas, and certain other of them, should go up to Jerusalem unto the apostles and elders about this question.*

1. THE PROBLEM WAS STATED

    A. The issue was a Jewish question which was entering into the Christian Church.

        Acts 15:5, *But there rose up certain of the sect of the Pharisees which believed, saying, That it was needful to circumcise them, and to command them to keep the law of Moses.*

    B. Peter recalled his ministry to Cornelius, the first gentile convert.

        Acts 15:7-8, *And when there had been much disputing, Peter rose up, and said unto them, Men and brethren, ye know how that a good while ago God made choice among us, that the Gentiles by my mouth should hear the word of the gospel, and believe.*
        v. 8, *And God, which knoweth the hearts, bare them witness, giving them the Holy Ghost, even as he did unto us:*

C.   Peter confessed that there was no difference between Jews and Gentiles.

Acts 15:9, *And put no difference between us and them, purifying their hearts by faith.*

2.   SALVATION IS THROUGH GRACE

A.   He further reminded them that salvation is a gift.

Acts 15:11, *But we believe that through the grace of the Lord Jesus Christ we shall be saved, even as they.*

B.   Peter said that demanding circumcision was tempting God.

Acts 15:10, *Now therefore why tempt ye God, to put a yoke upon the neck of the disciples, which neither our fathers nor we were able to bear?*

C.   Paul and Barnabas testified.

Acts 15:12, *Then all the multitude kept silence, and gave audience to Barnabas and Paul, declaring what miracles and wonders God had wrought among the Gentiles by them.*

3.   A DECISION IS REACHED

A.   James makes a judgment.

Acts 15:13, 19-21, *And after they had held their peace, James answered, saying, Men and brethren, hearken unto me:*

v. 19,   *Wherefore my sentence is, that we trouble not them, which from among the Gentiles are turned to God:*
v. 20,   *But that we write unto them, that they abstain from pollutions of idols, and from fornication, and from things strangled,a nd from blood.*
v. 21,   *For Moses of old time hath in every city them that preach him, being read in the synagogues every sabbath day.*

B.   The council is in agreement.

Acts 15:22, *Then pleased it the apostles and elders, with the shole church, to send chosen men of their own company to Antioch with Paul and Barnabas; namely, Judas surnamed Barsabas, and Silas, chief men among the brethren.*

C.   The decision was by the Holy Ghost.

Acts 15:28, *For it seemed good to the Holy Ghost, and to us, to lay upon you no greater burden than these necessary things.*

4. A LETTER IS SENT TO ALL THE CONGREGATION

A. It stated the verdict.

Acts 15:23-24, 28-29, *And they wrote letters by them after this manner; The apostles and elders and brethren send greeting unto the brethren which are of the Gentiles in Antioch and Syria and Cilicia:*
v. 24, *Forasmuch as we have heard, that certain which went out from us have troubled you with words, subverting your souls, saying, Ye must be circumcised, and keep the law: to whom we gave no such commandment:*

v. 28, *For it seemed good to the Holy Ghost, and to us, to lay upon you no greater burden than these necessary things;*
v. 29, *That ye abstain from meats offered to idols, and from blood, and from things strangled, and from fornication: from which if ye keep yourselves, ye shall do well, Fare ye well.*

B. It announced the arrival of men who could be more informative.

Acts 15:25-27, *It seemed good unto us, being assembled with one accord, to send chosen men unto you with our beloved Barnabas and Paul,*
v. 26, *Men that have hazarded their lives for the name of our Lord Jesus Christ.*
v. 27, *We have sent therefore Judas and Silas, who shall also tell you the same things by mouth.*

5. THE GENTILE MISSION CONTINUES

A. The message of Judas and Silas uplifted the hearts of the people.

Acts 15:30-33, *So when they were dismissed, they came to Antioch: and when they had gathered the multitude together, they delivered the epistle:*
v. 31, *Which when they had read, they rejoiced for the consolation.*
v. 32, *And Judas and Silas, being prophets also themselves, exhorted the brethren with many words, and confirmed them.*
v. 33, *And after they had tarried there a space, they were let go in peace from the brethren unto the apostles.*

B. When the others returned to Jerusalem, Silas, Barnabas, and Paul remained in Antioch ministering to the people.

Acts 15:34-35, *Notwithstanding it pleased Silas to abide there still.*
v. 35, *Paul also and Barnabas continued in Antioch, teaching and preaching the word of the Lord, with many others also.*

    C.   Paul and Barnabas decided to check on the churches they had started.

Acts 15:36, *And some days after Paul said unto Barnabas, Let us go again and visit our brethren in every city where we have preached the word of the Lord, and see how they do.*

6. PAUL AND BARNABAS SPLIT

    A.   The quarrel over whether or not to take John Mark with them separated the missionary team of Paul and Barnabas.

Acts 15:37-38, *And Barnabas determined to take with them John, whose surname was Mark.*
v. 38, But Paul thought not good to take him with them, who departed from them from Pamphylia, and went not with them to the work.

    B.   Barnabas and John Mark joined forces.

Acts 15:39, *And the contention was so sharp between them, that they departed asunder one from the other: and so Barnabas took Mark, and sailed unto Cyprus:*

    C.   Paul and Silas began traveling together.

Acts 15:40-41, *And Paul chose Silas, and departed, being recommended by the brethren unto the grace of God.*
v. 41, And he went through Syria and Cilicia, confirming the churches.

    D.   John Mark had deserted Paul on an earlier mission.

Acts 13:13, *Now when Paul and his company loosed from Paphos, they came to Perga in Pamphylia; and John departing from them returned to Jerusalem.*

    E.   Later he was reconciled to Paul.

II Timothy 4:11, *Only Luke is with me. Take Mark, and bring him with thee: for he is profitable to me for the ministry.*

STUDY GUIDE

INDIANA CHRISTIAN UNIVERSITY

THE ACTS OF THE APOSTLES

Lesson 22

THE CHURCH CONFRONTS PAGANISM

INTRODUCTION:

The gifts of the Spirit strengthened the Church with power and direction to confront a pagan world.

READING:

Acts 16:6, *Now when they had gone throughout Phygia and the region of Galatia, and were forbidden of the Holy Ghost to preach the word in Asia.*

1. THE DISCERNING OF SPIRITS

    A.   The Holy Spirit forbade Paul and his party to minister in Asia (Acts 16:6).

        1)   The gift of the discerning of spirits was in operation.

        2)   The Holy Spirit knew that the people were not ready to receive the gospel.

    B.   Next, Paul wished to go into Bithynia, but again the Holy Spirit forbade him.

    Acts 16:7, *After they were come to Mysia, they assayed to go into Bithynia: but the Spirit suffered them not.*

        1)   The gift of the discerning of spirits of men was in operation again.

        2)   The Holy Spirit was directing the spread of the gospel.

2.   THE GIFT OF THE WORD OF WISDOM

Acts 16:9-10, *And a vision appeared to Paul in the night; There stood a man of Macedonia, and prayed him, saying, Come over into Macedonia, and help us.*
v. 10, And after he had seen the vision, immediately we endeavoured to go into Macedonia, asssuredly gathering that the Lord had called us for to preach the gospel unto them.

A.   Paul received a revelation to go to Macedonia. Immediately, he obeyed.

B.   The gift of the word of wisdom was functioning to show Paul the future. The gospel would prosper in Macedonia.

3.   THE GIFT OF DISCERNING OF SPIRITS

A.   In Philippi, Macedonia, Paul came across a girl who was a fortuneteller.

Acts 16:16-17, *And it came to pass, as we went to prayer, a certain damsel possessed with a spirit of divination met us, which brought her masters much gain by soothsaying:*
v. 17, The same followed Paul and us, and cried, saying, These men are the servants of the most high God, which shew unto us the way of salvation.

B.   Paul cast out the spirit of divination.

Acts 16:18, *And this did she many days. But Paul, being grieved, turned and said to the spirit, I command thee in the name of Jesus Christ to come out of her. And he came out the same hour.*

C.   However, the girl's masters were ungrateful and unthankful.

Acts 16:19-21, *And when her masters saw that the hope of their gains was gone, they caught Paul and Silas, and drew them into the marketplace unto the rulers,*
v. 20, And brought them to the magistrates, saying, These men, being Jews, do exceedingly trouble our city,
v. 21, And teach customs, which are not lawful for us to receive, neither to observe, being Romans.

D.   They had Paul and Silas castigated, accused, beaten, and jailed.

Acts 16:22-24, *And the multitude rose up together against them: and the magistrates rent off their clothes, and commanded to beat them.*
v. 23, And when they had laid many stripes upon them, they cast them into prison, charging the jailer to keep them safely:
v. 24, Who, having received such a charge, thrust them into the inner prison, and made their feet fast in the stocks.

E.   There was conflict: God's power versus the devil's power. These Christians had the right spirit before the Lord when they were being persecuted.

Acts 16:25, *And at midnight Paul and Silas prayed, and sang praises unto God: and the prisoners heard them.*

1)   They sang and praised God at midnight while in prison.

2)   Their mistreatment, humiliation, and pain could not destroy God's love and peace.

4.   THE GIFT OF FAITH AND THE WORKING OF MIRACLES

A.   Paul could not do anything, but faith could. He had chains on his feet, but not on his faith. One effect of the functioning of the gift of faith was an unusual earthquake.

Acts 16:26, *And suddenly there was a great earthquake, so that the foundations of the prison were shaken: and immediately all the doors were opened, and everyone's bands were loosed.*

1)   And earthquake hit the jail and shook the foundations.

2)   The prisoners' chains fell off. This was not the work of an ordinary earthquake.

B.   As a result, the Philippian jailer and his family were saved.

1)   Believing all his prisoners had escaped, the keeper of the prison prepared to die.

Acts 16:27, *And the keeper of the prison awaking out of his sleep, and seeing the prison doors open, he drew out his sword, and would have killed himself, supposing that the prisoners had been fled.*

2)   Paul hastily reassured him that all his prisoners were still there.

Acts 16:28, *But Paul cried out with a loud voice, saying, Do thyself no harm: for we are all here.*

3)   Astonished, the man desired to know more about Paul's God. The functioning of the gifts of the Spirit made this man eager to know more about the Lord.

Acts 16:29-30, *Then he called for a light, and sprang in, and came trembling, and fell down before Paul and Silas,*
v. 30, *And brought them out, and said, Sirs, what must I do to be saved?*

4)   The disciples immediately taught them about Jesus.

Acts 16:31-33, *And they said, Believe on the Lord Jesus Christ, and thou shalt be saved, and thy house.*
v. 32, And they spake unto him the word of the Lord, and to all that were in his house.
v. 33, And he took them the same hour of the night, and washed their stripes; and was baptized, he and all his, straightway.

C.   Paul and Silas were respectfully escorted from prison by the authorities.

Acts 16:37-39, *But Paul said unto them, They have beaten us openly uncondemned, being Romans, and have cast us into prison; and now do they thrust us out privily? nay verily; but let them come themselves and fetch us out.*
v. 38, And the sergeants told these words unto the magistrates: and they feared, when they heard that they were Romans.
v. 39, And they came and besought them, and brought them out, and desired them to depart out of the city.

5.   THE CHURCH UNDER ATTACK

Although there are no recorded functionings of the gifts of the Spirit in this chapter, the Holy Spirit is mightily drawing men to salvation.

A.   Thessalonica

1)   An amazing revival begins at Thessalonica.

Acts 17:2, 4, *And Paul, as his manner was, went in unto them, and three sabbath days reasoned with them out of the scriptures,*
v. 4, And some of them believed, and consorted with Paul and Silas; and of the devout Greeks a great multitude, and of the chief women not a few.

2)   The leaders became angry about the power of God and about many who were getting converted.

Acts 17:5-6, *But the Jews which believed not, moved with envy, took unto them certain lewd fellows of the baser sort, and gathered a company, and set all the city on an uproar, and assaulted the house of Jason, and sought to bring them out to the people.*
v. 6, And when they found them not, they drew Jason and certain brethren unto the rulers of the city, crying, These that have turned the world upside down are come hither also;

The Church Confronts Paganism
Lesson 22

    B.   Berea

        1)   In Berea more souls were added as the people listened to the testimonies and searched the Scriptures to see of they could be true. The revival swept in great numbers of men.

            Acts 17:11-12, These were more noble than those in Thessalonica, in that they received the word with all readiness of mind, and searched the Scriptures daily, whether those things were so.
v. 12, Therefore many of them believed; also of honourable women which were Greeks, and of men, not a few.

        2)   There was also trouble in Berea. The wicked ones from Thessalonica came over and stirred up the people.

            Acts 17:13, But when the Jews of Thessalonica had knowledge that the word of God was preached of Paul at Berea, they came thither also, and stirred up the people.

    C.   Athens

        1)   While waiting for Silas and Timotheus at Athens, Paul rebuked false religion and preached the resurrection in Jewish temples, in the market place, and on Mars' Hill.

            Acts 17:16-17, 22, Now while Paul waited for them at Athens, his spirit was stirred in him, when he saw the city wholly given to idolatry.
v. 17, Therefore disputed he in the synagogue with the Jews, and with the devout persons, and in the market daily with them that met with him.
v. 22, Then Paul stood in the midst of Mars' hill, and said, Ye men of Athens, I perceive that in all things ye are too superstitious.

        2)   Some mocked him, and some wanted to hear about it at a later time, but certain men believed.

            Acts 17:32, 34, And when they heard of the resurrection of the dead, some mocked: and others said, We will hear thee again of this matter.

            v. 34, Howbeit certain men clave unto him, and believed: among the which was Dionysius the Areopagite, and a woman named Damaris, and others with them.

NOTES

_____

_____

_____

_____

_____

_____

_____

_____

_____

_____

_____

_____

_____

_____

_____

_____

_____

_____

_____

_____

_____

_____

_____

_____

_____

_____

_____

_____

STUDY GUIDE

INDIANA CHRISTIAN UNIVERSITY

THE ACTS OF THE APOSTLES

Lesson 23

THE CHURCH GROWS INTERNATIONALLY

INTRODUCTION:

Jesus had promised the disciples that the Holy Spirit would give them power to be witnesses to the ends of the earth. Here, we see the fulfillment in operation.

READING:

Acts 19:10, *And this continued by the space of two years; so that all they which dwelt in Asia heard the word of the Lord Jesus, both Jews and Greeks.*

1. THE LEADER OF THE SYNAGOGUE BELIEVED

    In Corinth a temple ruler became a believer.

    Acts 18:8, *And Crispus, the chief ruler of the synagogue, believed on the Lord with all his house; and many of the Corinthians hearing believed, and were baptized.*

2. THE WORD OF KNOWLEDGE OPERATED AT CORINTH

    Through the gift of the word of knowledge, God directed Paul to continue preaching in the city of Corinth.

    Acts 18:9-10, *Then spake the Lord to Paul in the night by a vision, Be not afraid, but speak, and hold not they peace:*
    v. 10, *For I am with thee, and no man shall set on thee to hurt thee: for I have much people in this city.*

    A. God promised that Paul would receive no hurt in Corinth.

    B. He revealed that He had many believers in that city.

    C. The knowledge was supernaturally imparted.

3. EPHESUS WAS A CENTER OF IDOLATRY

    A. Paul's next missionary journey took him to Ephesus, the largest city in the East at the time of Christ.

        1) It housed the Temple of Artemis, also known as Diana of the Ephesians. This is one of the seven wonders of the world.

        2) Additionally, the Temple of Bacchus was located in Ephesus.

    B. Paul walked up the Arcadian Way from his boat to the Great Theatre, a distance of about 500 yards.

        1) He passed shops of business on each side.

        2) The mammoth theatre seated 25,000 people.

4. THE EPHESIANS RECEIVE THE HOLY SPIRIT

At Ephesus Paul discovered disciples who were believers, but had never heard of the Holy Ghost.

Acts 19:1-2, 6, *And it came to pass, that, while Apollos was at Corinth, Paul having passed through the upper coasts came to Ephesus: and finding certain disciples,*
v. 2, *He said unto them, Have ye received the Holy Ghost since ye believed? And they said unto him, We have not so much as heard whether there be any Holy Ghost.*

v. 6, *And when Paul had laid his hands upon them, the Holy Ghost came on them; and they spake with tongues, and prophesied.*

    A. The Ephesians received the gift of speaking in other tongues.

    B. This occurred A.D. 54, or 21 years after the Jerusalem revival. The gift was not dead or cancelled.

    C. The Ephesians who received were already believers.

    D. They did not know about the Holy Spirit.

    E. Paul laid hands on them.

5. MASS DELIVERANCE WAS THE RESULT

Occult books, worth more than 50,000 pieces of silver, the price of 1,666 and • slaves, were burned publicly. When the Spirit of God moves, spiritism and demonism die.

Acts 19:19-20, *Many of them also which used curious arts brought their books together, and burned them before all men: and they counted the price of them, and found it fifty thousand pieces of silver.*
v. 20, *So mightily grew the word of God and prevailed.*

6. GIFTS OF HEALING OPERATED

Acts 19:11-12, *And God wrought special miracles by the hands of Paul:*
v. 12, *So that from his body were brought unto the sick handkerchiefs or aprons, and the diseases departed from them, and the evil spirits went out of them.*

A. People were healed when Paul laid hands on them.

B. Diseases and evil spirits were driven out when handkerchiefs that had touched Paul's body were laid on people. God used these material things as a point of contact for faith, but it was by His Spirit that humans were healed.

7. THE COUNTERFEIT FAILED

When you start doing something good, another person who does not have the same spirit as you will try to mimic you. It will not work.

A. Seven sons of a priest decided they would become exorcists after the manner of Paul.

Acts 19:13-16, *Then certain of the vagabond Jews, exorcists, took upon them to call over them which had evil spirits the name of the Lord Jesus, saying, We adjure you by Jesus whom Paul preacheth.*
v. 14, *And there were seven sons of one Sceva, a Jew, and chief of the priests, which did so.*
v. 15, *And the evil spirit answered and said, Jesus I know, and Paul I know; but who are ye?*
v. 16, *And the man in whom the evil spirit was leaped on them, and overcame them, and prevailed against them, so that they fled out of that house naked and wounded.*

B. Only blood-washed saints were able to operate the gifts of the Holy Spirit.

NOTES

STUDY GUIDE

INDIANA CHRISTIAN UNIVERSITY

THE ACTS OF THE APOSTLES

Lesson 24

PAUL RAISES THE DEAD AND DAUGHTERS WHO PROPHESY

INTRODUCTION:

In Acts chapters 20 and 21, we find that the gifts of the Spirit are very much alive. The date is A.D. 59, 26 years from the Day of Pentecost, and the Holy Spirit is powerfully operating, drawing men to God.

READING:

Acts 21:17, 19-20, *And when we were come to Jerusalem, the brethren received us gladly.*

v. 19, *And when he had saluted them, he declared particularly what things God had wrought among the Gentiles by his ministry.*
v. 20, *And when they heard it, they glorified the Lord. . .*

1.   THE GIFT OF THE WORKING OF MIRACLES

    A.   In the house where the believers were gathered together to hear Paul, a youth fell to his death.

        Acts 20:8-9, *And there were many lights in the upper chamber, where they were gathered together.*
        v. 9, *And there sat in a window a certain young man named Eutychus, being fallen into a deep sleep: and as Paul was long preaching, he sunk down with sleep, and fell down from the third loft, and was taken up dead.*

        1)   The young man was named Eutychus.

        2)   His name means "Fortunate!"

3)   He was fortunate in that:

a)   He was a young man.

b)   He knew Christ as his Savior.

c)   He sat under the direct ministry of Paul.

4)   The building was packed with people to the third floor.

5)   Eutychus was sitting in the window on the third floor when he fell asleep.

6)   As he "sunk down with sleep," he hurtled to his death.

2.   THE WORD OF WISDOM

The Holy Spirit revealed that as Paul journeyed to Jerusalem, in every city he would face imprisonment or beatings. He would be hounded and hated.

Acts 20:22-24, *And now, behold, I go bound in the spirit unto Jerusalem, not knowing the things that shall befall me there:*
v. 23, Save that the Holy Ghost witnesseth in every city, sying that bonds and afflictions abide me.
v. 24, But none of these things move me, neither count I my life dear unto myself, so that I might finish my course with joy, and the ministry, which I have received of the Lord Jesus, to testify the gospel of the grace of God.

A.   Paul was warned that he would be afflicted in every city.

B.   This revelation of the fututre was a function of the word of wisdom.

3.   ANOTHER WORD OF WISDOM

Again the Holy Spirit disclosed to Paul the destiny that awaited him in Jerusalem.

Acts 21:4-6, *And finding disciples, we tarried there seven days: who said to Paul through the Spirit, that he should not go up to Jerusalem.*
v. 5, And when we had accomplished those days, we departed and went our way; and they all brought us on our way, with wives and children, till we were out of the city: and we kneeled down on the shore, and prayed.
v. 6, And when we had taken our leave of one another, we took ship and they returned home again.

A. This time the word of wisdom functioned through some disciples who were simply church members.

B. This proves the gifts did not flow just through the hierarchy, but the gifts flowed through the total Body of Christ.

4. THE GIFT OF PROPHECY

Gifts of the Spirit functioned through women.

Acts 21:8-9, *And the next day we that were of Paul's company departed, and came unto Cæsarea: and we entered into the house of Philip the evangelist, which was one of the seven; and abode with him.*
v. 9, *And the same man had four daughters, virgins, which did prophesy.*

A. The gift of prophecy is a body ministry for the congregation.

   1) I Corinthians 14:3, *But he that prophesieth unto men to edification, and exhortation, and comfort.*

      a) It edifies.

      b) It exhorts.

      c) It comforts.

B. The four daughters of Philip all manifested this gift.

5. THE WORD OF WISDOM

A. The gift of the word of wisdom projected the futute for the Apostle through a certain prophet named Agabus.

Acts 21:10-11, *And as we tarried there many days, there came down from Judæa a certain prophet, named Agabus.*
v. 11, *And when he was come unto us, he took Paul's girdle, and bound his own hands and feet, and said, Thus saith the Holy Ghost, so shall the Jews at Jerusalem bind the man that owneth this girdle, and shall deliver him into the hands of the Gentiles.*

   1) Once more the Spirit advised Paul that he would be imprisoned when he reached Jerusalem.

   2) Additionally, he would be turned over to the Roman government.

B.   Paul did not count his life as something precious to be preserved at all costs.

Acts 21:12-13, *And when we heard these things, both we, and they of that place, besought him not to go up to Jerusalem.*
v. 13, *Then Paul answered, What mean ye to weep and to break mine heart? for I am ready not to be bound only, but also to die at Jerusalem for the name of the Lord Jesus.*

1)   Something inside of Paul said, "None of these things move me."

2)   He lived recklessly for the Lord, not for himself.

THE ACTS OF THE APOSTLES

Lesson 25

PAUL IN THE HANDS OF IMPERIAL ROME

INTRODUCTION:

The great apostle is nearing the end of his exciting public ministry; yet the operation of the Holy Spirit is still very powerful. The year is A.D. 60, 27 years after the day of Pentecost. No longer a baby, the Church has been grinding through empires for 27 years. By this time it has touched even the Cæsar's household.

READING:

Acts 23:11,*And the night following the Lord stood by him, and said, Be of good cheer, Paul: for as thou hast testified of me in Jerusalem, so must thou bear witness also at Rome.*

1. GIFTS OF THE SPIRIT WHICH DIRECTED PAUL'S LIFE

   A. Paul witnessed about the first time a word of wisdom came to him.

      Acts 22:6-11, *And it came to pass, that, as I made my journey, and was come nigh unto Damascus about noon, suddenly there shone from heaven a great light round about me.*
      v. 7, And I fell unto the ground, and heard a voice saying unto me, Saul, Saul, why persecutest thou me?
      v. 8, And I answered, Who art thou, Lord? And he said unto me, I am Jesus of Nazareth, whom thou persecutest.
      v. 9, And they that were with me saw indeed the light, and were afraid; but they heard not the voice of him that spake to me.
      v. 10, And I said, What shall I do, Lord? And the Lord said unto me, Arise, and go into Damascus; and there it shall be told thee of all things which are appointed for thee to do.
      v. 11, And when I could not see for the glory of that light, being led by the hand of them that were with me, I came to Damascus.

B. He described the functioning of one of the gifts of healing which restored his sight.

Acts 22:12-13, *And one Ananias, a devout man according to the law, having a good report of all the Jews which dwelt there,*
v. 13, Came unto me, and stood, and said unto me, Brother Saul, receive thy sight. And the same hour I looked up upon him.

C. He reminded his listeners of the word of wisdom which foretold that he, Paul, would be a witness for God. This was a graphic functioning of the word of wisdom.

Acts 22:14-16, *And he said, The God of our fathers hath chosen thee, that thou shouldest know his will, and see that Just One, and shouldest hear the voice of his mouth.*
v. 15, For thou shalt be his witness unto all men of what thou hast seen and heard.
v. 16, And now why tarriest thou? arise, and be baptized, and wash away thy sins, calling on the name of the Lord.

D. He recalled the operation of he gift of discerning of spirits. God revealed that these men would never receive this testimony.

Acts 22:17-18, *And it came to pass, that, when I was come again to Jerusalem, even while I prayed in the temple, I was in a trance;*
v. 18, And saw him saying unto me, Make haste, and get thee quickly out of Jerusalem: for they will not receive thy testimony concerning me.

E. Through a vision, Paul knew his future.

Acts 22:19-21, *And I said, Lord, they know that I imprisoned and beat in every synagogue them that believed on thee:*
v. 20, And when the blood of thy martyr Stephen was shed, I also was standing by, and consenting unto his death, and kept the raiment of them that slew him.
v. 21, And he said unto me, Depart: for I will send thee far hence unto the Gentiles.

1) For some reason, Paul remained in the city only to be arrested and imprisoned.

2) This fulfilled a number of prophecies, which is the function of the word of wisdom.

2. THE WORD OF WISDOM

Although some Jews had vowed not to eat or drink until they had killed Paul, God assured him that he would witness in Rome before he died.

Acts 23:11, *And the night following the Lord stood by him, and said, Be of good cheer, Paul: for as thou hast testified of me in Jerusalem, so must thou bear witness also at Rome.*

A.   The Lord stood by Paul and assured him he would minister in Rome, the headquarters of the Roman Empire.

B.   This meant that the Jews or the Roman soldiers could not kill him on the way to Rome. The prophecy must be fulfilled.

3. THE GOVERNOR HEARS HIS CASE

A.   The high priest took Tertullus, his prize orator, to build the argument against Paul.

Acts 24:5-9, *For we have found this man a pestilent fellow, and a mover of sedition among all the Jews throughout the world, and a ringleader of the sect of the Nazarenes:*
v. 6, Who also hath gone about to profane the temple: whom we took, and would have judged according to our law.
v. 7, But the chief captain Lysias came upon us, and with great violence took him away out of our hands,
v. 8, Commanding his accusers to come unto thee: by examining of whom thyself mayest take knowledge of all these things, whereof we accuse him.
v. 9, And the Jews also assented, saying that these things were so.

B.   Later, Felix heard Paul's side.

Acts 24:24-25, *And after certain days, when Felix came with his wife Drusilla, which was a Jewess, he sent for Paul, and heard him concerning the faith in Christ.*
v. 25, And as he reasoned of righteousness, temperance, and judgment to come, Felix trembled, and answered, Go thy way for this time; when I have a convenient season, I will call for thee.

This chapter ends with Paul still in prison.

4. PAUL APPEALS TO CAESAR

A. Festus traveled to Cæsarea to hear the complaints against Paul and invited him to be tried at Jerusalem.

Acts 25:6-9, *And when he had tarried among them more than ten days, he went down unto Cæsarea; and the next day sitting on the judgment seat commanded Paul to be brought.*
v. 7, *And when he was come, the Jews which came down from Jerusalem stood round about, and laid many and grievous complaints against Paul, which they could not prove.*
v. 8, *While he answered for himself, Neither against the law of the Jews, neither against the temple, nor yet against Cæsar, have I offended any thing at all.*
v. 9, *But Festus, willing to do the Jews a pleasure, answered Paul, and said, Wilt thou go up to Jerusalem, and there be judged of these things before me?*

B. Paul's reply was powerfully eloquent.

Acts 25:10-11, *Then said Paul, I stand at Cæsar's judgment seat, where I ought to be judged: to the Jews have I done no wrong, as thou very well knowest.*
v. 11, *For if I be an offender, or have committed any thing worthy of death, I refuse not to die: but if there be none of these things whereof these accuse me, no man may deliver me unto them. I appeal to Cæsar.*

5. PAUL'S DEFENSE BEFORE AGRIPPA

A. For the third time, Paul related his story to a judge.

Acts 26:19-23, *Whereupon, I king Agrippa, I was not disobedient unto the heavenly vision:*
v. 20, *But shewed first unto them of Damascus, and at Jerusalem, and throughout all the coasts of Judæa, and then to the Gentiles, that they should repent and turn to God, and do works meet for repentance.*
v. 21, *For these causes the Jews caught me in the temple, and went about to kill me.*
v. 22, *Having therefore obtained help of God, I continue unto this day, witnessing both to small and great, saying none other things than those which the prophets and Moses did say should come:*
v. 23, *That Christ should suffer, and that he should be the first that should rise from the dead, and should shew light unto the people, and to the Gentiles.*

B. Festus loudly interrupted.

Acts 26:24, And as he thus spake for himself, Festus said with a loud voice, Paul, thou art beside thyself; much learning doth make thee mad.

C. Paul graciously answered the governor.

Acts 26:25-27, But he said, I am not mad, most noble Festus; but speak forth the words of truth and soberness.
v. 26, For the king knoweth of these things, before whom also I speak freely: for I am persuaded that none of these things are hidden from him; for this thing was not done in a corner.
v. 27, King Agrippa, believest thou the prophets? I know that thou believest.

6. PAUL SAILS FOR ROME

The gift of the word of wisdom operated twice concerning this voyage.

A. Through Paul, God warned the men not to sail at that time.

Acts 27:20-21, And when neither sun nor stars in many days appeared, and no small tempest lay on us, all hope that we should be saved was then taken away.
v. 21, But after long abstinence Paul stood forth in the midst of them, and said, Sirs, ye should have hearkened unto me, and not have loosed from Crete, and to have gained this harm and loss.

B. When all hope was gone, an angel appeared with another word from God.

Acts 27:22-25, And now exhort you to be of good cheer: for there shall be no loss of any man's life among you, but of the ship.
v. 23, For there stood by me this night the angel of God, whose I am, and whom I serve.
v. 24, Saying, Fear not, Paul; thou must be brought before Cæsar: and, lo, God hath given thee all them that sail with thee.
v. 25, Wherefore, sirs, be of good cheer: for I believe God, that it shall be even as it was told me.

1) Every human would be saved.

2) The ship would sink.

3) Paul would stand before Cæsar.

NOTES

STUDY GUIDE

INDIANA CHRISTIAN UNIVERSITY

THE ACTS OF THE APOSTLES

Lesson 26

THE CHURCH MARCHES INTO THE FUTURE WITH MIRACLES

INTRODUCTION:

In Acts 28, there are two gifts in operation. We have now covered 30 to 33 years of time: a generation. The Church has grown up. It has members in many nations.

READING:

Acts 28:25, *And when they agreed not among themselves, they departed, after that Paul had spoken one word, Well spake the Holy Ghost by Esaias the prophet unto our fathers.*

1. THE GIFT OF WORKING OF MIRACLES

The gifts have not diminished.

Acts 28:3-6, *And when Paul had gathered a bundle of sticks, and laid them on the fire, there came a viper out of the heat, and fastened on his hand.*
v. 4, And when the barbarians saw the venomous beast hang on his hand, they said among themselves, No doubt this man is a murderer, whom, though he hath escaped the sea, yet vengence suffereth not to live.
v. 5, And he shook off the beast into the fire, and felt no harm.
v. 6, Howbeit they looked when he should have swollen, or falled down dead suddenly: but after they had looked a great while, and was not harm come to him, they changed their minds, and said that he was a god.

A.   The poisonous bite did not cause Paul to die immediately.

B.   He suffered no ill effects at all.

2. THE GIFTS OF HEALING

Healings were manifested as the disciples prayed and laid hands on people.

Acts 28:7-10, *In the same quarters were possessions of the chief man of the island, whose name was Publius; who received us, and lodged us three days courteously.*
v. 8, *And it came to pass, that the father of Publius lay sick of a fever and of a bloody flux: to whom Paul entered in, and prayed, and laid his hands on him, and healed him.*
v. 9, *So when this was done, others also, which had diseases in the island, came, and were healed:*
v. 10, *Who also honoured us with many honours; and when we departed, they laded us with such things as were necessary.*

A. The father of the island's governor was healed of a fever and internal bleeding.

B. Others from the island were freed from diseases.

C. The grateful men and women honored them and supplied their needs.

D. When he finally reached Rome, Paul was able to lease a house where he could freely teach things which concerned the Lord Jesus Christ, with all confidence, no man forbidding him.

3. ACTS 29 -- THE GLORIOUS CHURCH WITH GIFTS UNTIL CHRIST RETURNS

A. Acts 29 is not in our Bible. It is in our hearts.

B. As Acts 28 closed 33 years after Acts 1, God began Acts 29. This is your chapter!

C. Nero's axe could not silence the Church at Paul's martyrdom.

D. The conquering legions of Rome could not silence the voice of the Church.

E. The Roman Forum could not legislate the defeat of the Acts of the Church.

F. The date of Acts 29 extends from A.D. 33 toward A.D. 2000.

4. PAUL BEARS WITNESS OF THE GIFTS OF THE SPIRIT IN OPERATION

Romans 15:16-19, *That I should be the minister of Jesus Christ to the Gentiles, ministering the gospel of God, that the offering up of the Gentiles might be acceptable, being sanctified by the Holy Ghost.*
v. 17, I have therefore whereof I may glory through Jesus Christ in those things which pertain to God.
v. 18, For I will not dare to speak of any of these things which Christ hath not wrought by me, to make the Gentiles obedient, by word and deed.
v. 19, Through mighty signs and wonders, by the power of the Spirit of God; so that from Jerusalem, and round about Illyricum, I have fully preached the gospel of Christ.

A. The mighty signs and wonders made the nations obedient to the Gospel.

B. It was done by "word and deed."

5. THE GIFTS OF THE SPIRIT WERE FUNCTIONING IN THE SECOND AND THIRD CENTURIES

A. In his *History Of The Apostolic Church* Book I, section 55, Dr. Philip Schaff writes:
"The speaking with tongues, however, was not confined to the day of Pentecost. Together with the other extraordinary spiritual gifts which distinguished this age above the succeeding periods of more quiet and natural development, this gift also thought to be sure in a modified form, perpetuated itself in the apostolic church. We find traces of it still in the second and third centuries."

B. Irenaeus (115 to 202 A.D.) was a pupil of Polycarp, who was a disciple of the Apostle John. He wrote in this book *Against the Heresies*, Book V, Part 40:
"In like manner do we also hear many brethren in the Church who possess prophetic gifts, and who through the Spirit speak all kinds of languages, and bring to light for the general benefit the hidden things of men and declare the mysteries of God, whom also the apostles term spiritual."

1) Irenaeus was a pupil of Polycarp.

2) Polycarp was a disciple of the Apostle John.

3) At least two generations later the gifts are still operating.

    C.   Tertullian (160-220 A.D.) invited Marcion to produce anything among his followers such as was common among the orthodox Christians: "Let him exhibit prophets such as have spoken, not by human sense but with the Spirit of God, such as have predicted things to come, and have made manifest the secrets of the heart; let him produce a psalm, a vision, a prayer, only let it be by the Spirit in an ecstasy, that is in a rapture, whenever an interpretation of tongues has occurred to him." He also gives a full description of a certain sister who often spoke with tongues. See Smith's Dictionary of the Bible, Vol. 4, Pg. 3310.

6.   THE GIFTS MANIFESTED IN THE FOURTH AND FIFTH CENTURIES

Augustine (354-430 A.D.) wrote: "We still do what the apostles did when they laid hands on the Samaritans and called down the Holy Spirit on them by the laying on of hands. It is expected that converts should speak with new tongues."

7.   THE GIFTS OF THE HOLY SPIRIT WERE ALIVE IN THE SIXTEENTH CENTURY

    A.   In the *History Of The Christian Church* by Philip Schaff, we read of Vincent Ferrer who died in 1419. Spondamus and many others say this saint was honored with the gift of tongues.

    B.   In a German work, Souer's *History Of The Christian Church*, Vol. 3, page 406, the following is found: "Dr. Martin Luther (1483-1546) was a prophet, evangelist, speaker in tongues and interpreter, in one person, endowed with all gifts of the Holy Spirit."

STUDY GUIDE

INDIANA CHRISTIAN UNIVERSITY

THE ACTS OF THE APOSTLES

Lesson 27

THE HOLY SPIRIT AND THE CHURCH, PAST & PRESENT

INTRODUCTION:

The gifts of the Holy Spirit were the dynamics of the newborn church. They were not confined to the first generation of believers or the apostles. The gifts of the Holy Spirit were never limited to just the apostles.

READING:

I Corinthians 12:8-11, *For to one is given by the Spirit the word of wisdom; to another the word of knowledge by the same Spirit;*
v. 9, *To another faith by the same Spirit; to another the gifts of healing by the same Spirit;*
v. 10, *To another the working of miracles; to another prophecy; to another discerning of spirits; to another divers kinds of tongues; to another the interpretation of tongues:*
v. 11, *But all these worketh that one and the selfsame Spirit, dividing to every man severally as he will.*

1.　NINE GIFTS OF THE HOLY SPIRIT

    A.　There are nine supernatural gifts of the Holy Spirit. They are three plus three plus three, or perfection (three) times perfection.

        1)　Three gifts of revelation

            a)　The word of wisdom
            b)　The word of knowledge
            c)　The discerning of spirits

        2)　Three gifts of power

            a)　The working of miracles
            b)　Faith
            c)　The gifts of healings

3) Three gifts of inspiration

    a) Prophecy
    b) Diverse kinds of tongues
    c) Interpretation

2. WHICH GIFTS OF THE HOLY SPIRIT OPERATED IN THE EARLY CHURCH?

All nine gifts operated through the early church.

3. HOW OFTEN DID THE GIFTS OPERATE IN ACTS?

A. The book of Acts records over 50 distinct occasions where the gifts were manifested.

B. The gifts of the Holy Spirit operated in every chapter of Acts; unless a very long sermon was being preached, or a problem occurred in the church.

4. THE GIFTS DID NOT ONLY FUNCTION THROUGH HUMAN BEINGS

The gifts functioned through divinity.

A. Jesus

Acts 1:4, *And, being assembled together with them, commanded them that they should not depart from Jerusalem, but wait for the promise of the Father, which, saith he, ye have heard of me.*

B. Angels

Acts 1:11, *Which also said, Ye men of Galilee, why stand ye gazing up into heaven? this same Jesus, which is taken up from you into heaven, shall so come in like manner as ye have seen him go into heaven.*

C. The Holy Spirit

Acts 19:2-5, *He said unto them, Have ye received the Holy Ghost since ye believed? And they said unto him, We have not so much as heard whether there be any Holy Ghost.*
v. 3, And he said unto them, Unto what then were ye baptized? And they said, Unto John's baptism.
v. 4, Then said Paul, John verily baptized with the baptism of repentance, saying unto the people, that they should believe on him which should come after him, that is, on Christ Jesus.
v. 5, When they heard this, they were baptized in the name of the Lord Jesus.

5. WOMEN AND THE GIFTS OF THE HOLY SPIRIT

    A.   Mary and other women were filled with the Holy Spirit at Pentecost.

        Acts 1:14, *These all continued with one accord in prayer and supplication, with the women, and Mary the mother of Jesus, and with his brethren.*

    B.   Philip's daughters prophesied.

        Acts 21:9, *And the same man had four daughters, virgins, which did prophesy.*

6. LAYMEN AND THE GIFTS OF THE HOLY SPIRIT

    A.   There were 120 people in the Upper Room on the Day of Pentecost. Of these people, fewer than 12 were apostles. At least 108 laymen received the baptism of the Holy Spirit that day.

    B.   Stephen, a deacon, was the first martyr.

        Acts 7:59, *And they stoned Stephen, calling upon God, and saying, Lord Jesus, receive my spirit.*

    C.   Philip, another deacon, was translated to another place by the Spirit.

        Acts 8:39-40, *And when they were come up out of the water, the Spirit of the Lord caught away Philip, that the eunuch saw him no more: and he went on his way rejoicing.*
        v. 40, *But Philip was found at Azotus: and passing through he preached in all the cities, till he came to Caesarea.*

    D.   Ananias of Damascus prayed for Saul's healing.

        Acts 9:17, *And Ananias went his way, and entered into the house; and putting his hands on him said, Brother Saul, the Lord, even Jesus, that appeared unto thee in the way as thou camest, hath sent me, that thou mightest receive thy sight, and be filled with the Holy Ghost.*

    E.   The disciples in Lystria.

        Acts 14:19-20, *And there came thither certain Jews from Antioch and Iconium, who persuaded the people, and, having stoned Paul, drew him out of the city, supposing he had been dead.*
        v. 20, *Howbeit, as the disciples stood round about him, he rose up, and came into the city: and the next day he departed with Barnabas to Derbe.*

7. THE EARLY CHURCH WAS HELPED BY THE HOLY SPIRIT

A.   The Holy Spirit changed Peter from a backslider to a dynamic witness.

B.   He relieved Thomas of his doubts.

C.   The Holy Spirit delivered James and John from hunger for power.

D.   He changed Saul, the persecutor, to Paul, the apostle.

E.   He led the missionaries of the early church to the ends of the earth.

F.   He changed Greek pantheists to Christian believers.

G.   The Holy Spirit changed idol-worshipers in Caesar's household to believers in Jesus Christ.

H.   He turned Mary's mourning into rejoicing.

8. THE LIMITS ON THE GIFTS OF THE HOLY SPIRIT

A.   There is no limit to the number of gifts of the Holy Spirit a person may receive.

B.   There is no expiration date for the gifts of the Holy Spirit. They were not limited to the apostles and the early church.

Acts 2:39, *For the promise is unto you, and to your children, and to all that are afar off, even as many as the Lord our God shall call.*

9. OCCURRENCES OF THE OPERATION OF THE HOLY SPIIRT IN THE BOOK OF ACTS

No.	Where Recorded	Name of the Gift	Manifested Through
1.	Acts 1:4-5	Word of Wisdom	Jesus
2.	Acts 1:8	Word of Wisdom	Jesus
3.	Acts 1:11	Word of Wisdom	Angels
4.	Acts 2:4	Tongues	The 120
5.	Acts 2:39	Word of Wisdom	Peter
6.	Acts 2:43	Healing	All the Apostles
7.	Acts 2:43	Working of Miracles	All the Apostles

No.	Where Recorded	Name of Gift	Manifested Through
8.	Acts 3:6	Healing	Peter
9.	Acts 4:31	Faith	The Church
10.	Acts 5:3, 9	Discerning of Spirits	Peter
11.	Acts 5:12	Working of Miracles	All the Apostles
12.	Acts 5:15	Healing	All the Apostles, Peter's Shadow
13.	Acts 5:16	Healing	All the Apostles
14.	Acts 5:19	Working of Miracles	An Angel
15.	Acts 6:8	Working of Miracles	Stephen
		Healing	Stephen
16.	Acts 8:4-8	Healing	Philip
17.	Acts 8:13	Working of Miracles	Philip
18.	Acts 8:39	Working of Miracles	For Philip
19.	Acts 9:5	Working of Miracles	Jesus
20.	Acts 9:6	Word of Wisdom	Jesus
21.	Acts 9:8	Working of Miracles	Jesus
22.	Acts 9:17	Healing	Ananias
23.	Acts 9:34	Healing	Peter
24.	Acts 9:40	Healing	Peter
25.	Acts 10:1-8	Word of Knowledge	An Angel
26.	Acts 10:19	Word of Knowledge	Peter
27.	Acts 10:44	Speaking With Other Tongues	Cornelius' Household
28.	Acts 11:12	Word of Knowledge	Peter
29.	Acts 12:7-8	Faith	An Angel
30.	Acts 13:1-3	Prophecy	Barnabas, Simeon
31.	Acts 13:11	Working of Miracles	Paul
32.	Acts 14:3	Working of Miracles	The Apostles
33.	Acts 14:8-10	Healing	Paul
34.	Acts 14:19-20	Working of Miracles	The Disciples
35.	Acts 16:6	Discerning of Spirits	Holy Spirit
36.	Acts 16:9	Word of Wisdom	Paul
37.	Acts 16:16-18	Working of Miracles	Paul
38.	Acts 16:26	Working of Miracles	Paul
39.	Acts 18:9-11	Word of Knowledge	Paul
40.	Acts 19:6	Various Tongues	Disciples at Ephesus
41.	Acts 19:11	Working of Miracles	Paul
42.	Acts 20:9-10	Working of Miracles	Paul
43.	Acts 20:22-24	Word of Wisdom	Holy Spirit
44.	Acts 21:4-6	Word of Wisdom	The Church
45.	Acts 21:9	Prophecy	Four Daughters of Philip

The Holy Spirit and the Church, Past & Present
Lesson 27

No.	Where Recorded	Name of Gift	Manifested Through
46.	Acts 21:10	Word of Wisdom	Agabus
47.	Acts 22:17-18	Word of Wisdom	Paul
48.	Acts 23:11	Word of Wisdom	The Lord
49.	Acts 27:21-26	Word of Wisdom	Paul
50.	Acts 28:3-5	Working of Miracles	Paul
51.	Acts 28:8-9	Healing	Paul
52.	Acts 29	All Nine	The Total Church

ICU
Indiana Christian University

Bringing Quality Education To Your Home

In the last several years, educators around the country, including all of us here at Indiana Christian University, have seen a definite new trend in education. More and more, education is becoming decentralized and less campus-focused. This trend seems to be true in all areas of education, and especially in college work.

We here at ICU are very thankful that God has allowed us to be more than trend observers; we have been trendsetters. Because of his vision, insight and forethought--or should we say "prophetic knowledge"--Dr. Lester Sumrall developed a Bible curriculum which we can offer to the world through audio correspondence studies and video extension campuses. Due to his continuous travels as an evangelist and missionary during the years that he was trying to obtain his college education, Dr. Sumrall became acutely aware of the fact that traditional campus-based education would prove increasingly impractical for a greater number of people as their lives became more and more mobile. With this keen insight, Dr. Sumrall worked tirelessly to produce a college system that could go with the student rather than demanding that the student abandon his mission for a period of years to be anchored to a desk. The result was an off-campus program that makes Indiana Christian University literally a school with a global campus.

This correspondence program has allowed us to provide degree programs to ministers who cannot leave their churches, housewives who must stay with their families, missionaries in isolated mission posts, inmates in correctional institutions, patients in long-term medical facilities--and the list goes on and on.

In breaking beyond the limitation of our walls, ICU has begun to fulfill not only Dr. Sumrall's mandate, but also the directive left to us by Jesus Christ Himself: "Go ye therefore, and teach all nations..." (Matthew 28:19).

Introducing Indiana Christian University

Indiana Christian University is an independent school of higher learning serving all religious denominations. The student body and faculty reflect various types of church backgrounds, rather than any one denomination. The university is incorporated in the state of Indiana and grants degrees to those who satisfactorily complete the prescribed course of study.

The school's history dates to 1907, when a group of Christian people formed an institution for teaching the Bible and Bible-related subjects. It was chartered in the state of Indiana in 1923 as Indiana Bible Institute, becoming Indiana Bible College in 1934. The present name was adopted in 1940.

In addition to training ministers and professional people, the school has helped thousands of Christian laypeople gain a greater understanding of the Bible and has prepared them for Christian life. ICU became part of the Lester Sumrall Evangelistic Association in 1988. In 1990, the school was relocated from Indianapolis to its present home in South Bend. A merger with the former World Harvest Bible College was finalized in 1993, resulting in two campuses: Indianapolis and South Bend.

Programs of Study

A Certificate of Achievement in Charismatic Studies is awarded to students who successfully complete the basic curriculum of charismatic studies with a grade average of 2.00 (C) or better. The basic curriculum includes: Faith, English, Christian Foundations, The Total Man, Human Illness and Divine Healing, Demon Power, The Gifts of the Holy Spirit, Prayer, and four hours of Practicum.

The Associate of Arts in Christian Ministry and Bachelor of Arts in Christian Ministry are awarded to students who:

1. Demonstrate a Christian character which the school can recommend.
2. Complete the prescribed course (56 credit hours for the Associate of Arts in Christian Ministry program; 112 credit hours for the Bachelor of Arts in Christian Ministry program) with a grade average of 2.00 (C) or better.

	Associate of Arts in Christian Ministry	Bachelor of Arts in Christian Ministry
Language Department		
English	3 hrs.	3 hrs.
Bible Department		
Old Testament	6 hrs.	16 hrs.
New Testament	6 hrs.	16 hrs.
Theology Department-must include the courses listed for the certificate program	21 hrs.	21 hrs.
Ministry Department		
Practicum	8 hrs.	16 hrs.
History Department	3 hrs.	6 hrs.
Electives	9 hrs.	34 hrs.

Earn College Credit
For This Course Through

1. Complete the application process.

    a) Complete and mail the application form along with the $25 application fee.

    b) Request your high school and/or college(s) to mail transcripts to ICU.

    c) Give the Pastor's Reference Form to your pastor and request that it be returned directly to ICU.

    d) In order to request consideration for life experience for practicum credits, submit a full resume showing dates of ministry and full responsibilities involved. Verification from an overseer or other recognizable authority must accompany each ministry assignment.

2. Upon acceptance you will receive:

    a) a transcript indicating any coursework which has been transferred from previous institutions, or life experience.

    b) a study plan indicating the ICU courses recommended to complete the program of study you are enrolling into. Be sure to keep this guideline and follow it carefully.

    c) a registration form for registering for your courses.

    d) a Sumrall Publications catalog for ordering your class study materials and tapes.

    e) a "How to Write a Term Paper" manual.

3. Complete the registration form and return it along with the appropriate fee to ICU.

4. Complete the order form for your class study materials and tapes and return it along with the proper payment to Sumrall Publishing.

5. When your class study materials and tapes arrive, read the lessons and listen to the tapes in the way most helpful to you. It is suggested that you read the lesson once, listen to the tape, and then read the lesson again. Complete the test which will be mailed to you upon the submission of your class registration. Carefully following the instructions in the term paper manual, write and submit a term paper on a topic related to the course. The paper should be 10-12 double-spaced, typewritten pages. Font size should not exceed 14 points and margins should not exceed 1 1/2 inches. All information from source material must be properly footnoted and listed in a bibliography.